Dinner Party DESSERTS

Foreword by Arne Krüger

Macdonald

A **Macdonald** BOOK

Translated by Caroline Beamish
Copyright © 1981 Shogakukan Publishing Co. Ltd., Tokyo for the original edition
Copyright © 1983 Arnoldo Mondadori Editore S.p.A., Milan for the international edition
English translation copyright © 1984 Arnoldo Mondadori Editore S.p.A., Milan

First published in Great Britain in 1984
by Macdonald & Co (Publishers) Ltd
London & Sydney

A member of BPCC plc

British Library Cataloguing in Publication Data

Dinner party desserts
  1 Desserts
  I Faorenc, Napo
  641.8'6   TX773

  ISBN 0 356 10515 6

Printed and bound in Italy
by Officine Grafiche A. Mondadori Editore, Verona

Macdonald & Co (Publishers) Ltd
Maxwell House
74 Worship Street
London EC2A 2EN

Dinner Party
DESSERTS

Birthday cake

For the sponge: 4 oz/125 g sugar • 3 egg yolks • 3 egg whites • 4 oz/125 g flour • 1 tbsp Cointreau or Grand Marnier • few drops vanilla essence
For the raspberry filling: 2¼ oz/60 g raspberry jam or jelly • 1-2 tbsp lemon juice
For the Chantilly cream: 7 fl oz/200 ml double cream • 1 oz/25 g icing sugar
For the coffee buttercream: 7 oz/200 g butter • 1¼ oz/35 g icing sugar • 2 egg yolks • 4 tbsp strong black coffee
To garnish: 2 oz/50 g chocolate flakes

1 Prepare the sponge (*see* page 19, steps 1-4) using the quantities given above and adding the liqueur. Cut it into three layers.

2 Warm, then sieve the raspberry jam and mix in the lemon juice. Spread half the jam on the first layer of sponge. Spread half the Chantilly cream (*see* page 190) on top of the raspberry jam.

3 Cover the first layer of sponge with the second and repeat the filling in the same order, using the remaining jam and Chantilly cream.

4 Cover with the third layer of sponge. Spread the entire cake with three-quarters of the coffee buttercream (*see* page 19, steps 5 and 6).

5 Fit a piping bag with a plain nozzle and fill with the remaining coffee buttercream; decorate the top of the cake with two circles of rosettes and the sides of the cake and the space between the two circles of rosettes with chocolate flakes. Serve immediately, or store in the refrigerator.

and croissants, and also biscuits to accompany ice-cream, or to serve with coffee or tea.

Desserts are once again in fashion and the best are to be found in good restaurants everywhere: the great choice of desserts now offered is a measure of the gastronomic success they have achieved. How can this success be explained at a time when calorie counting has become an obsession? Sociologists and dietologists alone can tell. Nowadays restaurateurs and their pastry-cooks are able to offer their clients a hitherto unknown array of sweets. The traditional dessert trolley is laden with bowls, individual dishes and glasses, with all you could wish for, from kiwi fruit jelly to bilberry tart. One is quite simply spoilt for choice.

Whether you use this book at home, for entertaining friends or to make a special treat for the family you will produce desserts to be proud of.

Arne Krüger

Cakes and desserts for special occasions

the recipe. The reader should only substitute ingredients if a particular item is unobtainable. Cutting corners for reasons of economy, for example, rarely works where desserts are concerned. Butter, cream, best quality flour, sugar, walnuts and almonds are all essential ingredients to keep at hand in the store cupboard and the quality of these basic materials is of prime importance.

Many amateur cooks set themselves professional standards and spare no expense in the name of perfection. Moulds and special utensils can be found for the most complex creations; specialist shops stock all the necessary equipment, including sugar thermometers, to ensure that the sugar syrup reaches exactly the right temperature; moulds and patty tins in all shapes and sizes; wire racks on which tiny sweetmeats can be covered with chocolate and smaller moulds in a variety of shapes for making cold desserts, jellied sweetmeats, fondants, marzipan figures and petits fours.

All decorations are designed, however, to have a purely visual appeal; of greater importance are flavour and texture, which can only be perfected if the recipe is followed exactly and the ingredients measured with the greatest care. Some pastries should be crisp, some flaky, some should melt in the mouth; others must be firm enough to contain confectioner's custard or whipped cream. Some desserts are exceptionally light and frothy, others are substantial and extremely filling. Basic recipes can be modified to a certain extent – though the final product should retain the distinctive characteristics which give the dessert its particular name.

Attention must be paid not only to the quantity but also to the quality of the ingredients – choose only the best: the finest flour, caster sugar, fresh, ripe fruit, best quality butter, full-cream milk, fresh eggs and so on.

Kitchen utensils and pans must be spotlessly clean. It is a well-known fact for example, that it is impossible to whip egg whites in a bowl which contains even the slightest trace of grease. Moulds must be carefully cleaned after use and all utensils must be washed in plenty of hot water, preferably without detergent and carefully rinsed until all traces of food have disappeared. This may seem natural and obvious but the most rigorous self-discipline is essential to the art of the pastry-cook.

What is valid for the professional chef or confectioner is also valid for the amateur cook. Just as the professional has his or her customers to satisfy, so the cook at home must live up to the expectations of family and friends and create a good impression on the guests; the extra effort will be greatly appreciated.

This highly attractive book is the gourmet's delight, and includes internationally famous cakes and desserts. The professional pastry-cook and confectioner has always occupied a place of honour in the civilized world and confectionery as an art has been influenced from places as far away as China, the Arab world and Russia. The recipes in this collection include masterpieces of the confectioner's art, developed over centuries. Also included are other products which are not strictly speaking desserts, such as cheesecakes, scones, brioches

To delight the eye and please the palate

The art of the pastry-cook, the confectioner and the ice-cream maker is a fascinating subject both for the expert and the beginner. Confectioners traditionally command great respect thanks to the reputation of their illustrious predecessors, and thanks also to the vast number of recipes and methods of decorating confectionery accepted as part of the classic repertoire. Confectioners and pastry-cooks welcome new trends in their art but at the same time they are intent on preserving traditional methods and practices. The decoration of the finished product, however, is of supreme importance. Sweet flowers and candied fruit are   specially manufactured for decorating cakes and pastries; a wide variety of tiny masterpieces in pastry, praline or marzipan in their finely pleated paper cases tempt both the eye and the palate; rosettes, stars, scrolls and flourishes are patiently reproduced with syringe and nozzle to delight the eye of the consumer.

In comparison, the art of making desserts is on a slightly different and necessarily more modest scale. Desserts are intended and produced to be eaten rapidly. The flavour of the dessert must harmonize with and complement the courses that have preceded it: it must be an integral part of the whole meal. The visual element is often a matter of secondary importance: very often a dessert will consist of something baked and served in the same dish, or of individual portions of zabaione or mousse, whipped up at the last minute, none of which requires elaborate decoration. Ice-creams and sorbets can be simply served with a wafer or biscuit, or perhaps a rosette of whipped cream. Creams and gâteaux are more fashionable than ever today and make a fitting end to any meal.

Thanks to air transport, the most exotic varieties of fruit are widely available, providing a useful complement to seasonal home-grown fruits. Then there are the new hybrid varieties, which can be transformed into delicate jellies, mousses and sorbets or combined with other fruits, providing cooks with new and unusual flavours. Fruit purées can be used as sauces for creams and mousses, or can be mixed with liqueurs and served with fruit salads and ice-creams. Recipes and methods for making basic pastries and doughs have remained more or less unchanged over the years; ingredients must be measured exactly and the time-honoured principles or the 'science of cookery' must be adhered to even though the emphasis today may seem to point towards the importance of decorative techniques and the actual presentation of the finished creation.

Readers are advised to weigh all dry ingredients carefully, to measure liquids exactly and to use only the ingredients suggested in

Using this book
Measurements are given in imperial and metric.
Since conversions are working approximations only do not mix the two systems.

Plain flour is used throughout unless otherwise specified.

Contents

Snow cake

1 sponge 2½ in/6 cm thick and 7-8 in/18-20 cm in diameter ● (see page 19, steps 1-4) ● brandy to soak sponge
For the custard filling (steps 1-4): 8 fl oz/225 ml milk ● 2 oz/50 g sugar ● 2 egg yolks ● juice and grated rind of 1 orange ● 2 tbsp Curaçao ● 4 tbsp Grand Marnier
For the Chantilly cream: 18 fl oz/500 ml double cream ● 2½ oz/70 g icing sugar ● 2 tbsp brandy

1 Heat the milk and sugar gently to dissolve the sugar but do not allow to boil. Leave to cool slightly.

2 Beat the egg yolks. Add the milk and sugar from step 1.

3 Return this mixture to the saucepan and stir constantly. Remove from the heat just before boiling point is reached. The custard should have thickened sufficiently to coat the back of a spoon.

4 Add the orange juice and grated rind, the Curaçao and 2 tbsp of Grand Marnier.

5 Cut the sponge into three equal layers. Sprinkle with the remaining Grand Marnier. Spoon half the custard filling on to the first layer of cake.

6 Cover the first layer with the second layer of sponge and spoon over the remaining custard. Place the third layer of sponge on top and cover with the Chantilly cream (see page 190) flavoured with brandy. Use a piping bag to decorate the cake as desired.

Strawberry cream gâteau

1 sponge (see page 19, steps 1-4) ● Grand Marnier or Maraschino to soak sponge ● 14 oz/400 g strawberries
For the Chantilly cream: 14 fl oz/400 ml double cream ● 2 oz/50 g icing sugar

1 Prepare the sponge using the quantities given on page 19.

2 When the cake has cooled cut it into three equal layers. Sprinkle each layer with the liqueur of your choice.

3 Spread the first layer of sponge with Chantilly cream (page 190); cover with halved strawberries.

4 Place the second layer of sponge over the first and cover with more cream and strawberries.

5 Cover the second layer of sponge with the third layer.

6 Cover the entire cake with Chantilly cream and decorate with cream, using a piping bag. Decorate the top and sides with the remaining strawberries.

Prince Leopold cake

(Chocolate cake)

For the cake: 3 oz/80 g butter • 5 oz/150 g sugar • 8 egg yolks • 6 oz/175 g ground almonds • 7 oz/200 g grated chocolate • 2¾ oz/75 g flour • 3 tbsp rum • 8 egg whites • butter or margarine to grease cake tin
For the filling: 4 oz/125 g grated chocolate, melted • 18 fl oz/500 ml double cream • 2 level tbsp vanilla sugar

1 Cream the butter, sugar and egg yolks together in a bowl.

2 Fold in the ground almonds, grated chocolate, flour and rum.

3 In a separate bowl whip the egg whites until stiff and fold into the mixture.

4 Grease a spring-release cake tin. Pour the mixture into the tin and place in a preheated oven at 400°F/200°C/mark 6 for 45 minutes.

5 Remove the cake from the oven, turn out on to a wire rack and allow to cool.

6 Use a spoon to hollow out the centre of the cake; leave the base and sides not more than ¾ in/2 cm thick. Alternatively cut the cake into two or three layers.

7 To prepare the filling, crumble the removed centre of the cake as finely as possible and place the crumbs in the oven to crisp for 5-10 minutes. Do not allow to burn.

8 Mix the toasted cake crumbs with the melted grated chocolate. Whip the cream with the vanilla sugar, then fold in the crumb and chocolate mixture.

9 Fill the hollowed-out cake with the cream, covering the sides as well. Alternatively cover each layer as well as the top and the sides of the cake with cream (quantities of cream and chocolate will probably need to be increased in this case).

10 Place in the refrigerator for at least 1 hour before serving.

Coffee cream cake

For the sponge (steps 1-4): 6 oz/175 g sugar ● 6 egg yolks ● 6 egg whites ● 5½ oz/160 g flour (or 3½ oz/100 g flour and 2 oz/60 g cornflour) ● few drops vanilla essence ● coffee liqueur to soak sponge ● butter to grease and flour to dust cake tin
For the coffee buttercream (steps 5 and 6): 7oz/200 g butter ● 5½ oz/160 g icing sugar ● 2 egg yolks ● 2 tbsp instant coffee (or 3 tbsp strong black coffee) ● few drops vanilla essence
For decoration: 3½ oz/100 g toasted flaked almonds ● 1 tbsp cocoa powder

An almond-flavoured sponge can be made by following steps 1-4 on the opposite page, substituting ground almonds (see page 192) for the flour. (This is used in several recipes, for example on page 25.)

18

1 Beat together the sugar and egg yolks, standing the bowl over a bowl of hot water.

2 Whip the egg whites until stiff and fold gently into the sugar and egg yolk mixture.

3 Sift the flour and fold with the vanilla essence into the mixture.

4 Butter a cake tin and dust with flour. Pour the mixture into the tin. Place in a preheated oven at 325°F/170°C/mark 3 for 40 minutes.

5 For the buttercream make a sugar syrup with the icing sugar and a little water, allow it to cool, then add it to the egg yolks.

6 Cream the butter and stir in the mixture from step 5. Add the coffee, and mix again.

7 Cut the sponge into three equal layers. Using a pastry brush, brush the layers with coffee liqueur. Spread each layer with coffee buttercream, then cover the entire cake with the remaining cream.

8 Press toasted flaked almonds around the sides of the cake. Decorate the top with cocoa powder: place strips of paper diagonally across the cake in a lattice pattern, as illustrated; sieve the cocoa powder over the surface and remove the paper strips.

Chocolate mousse cake

For the sponge (steps 1-4): 3 eggs ● 3½ oz/100 g sugar ● 1¼ oz/ 35 g cocoa powder ● 2 tbsp hot water ● 1½ oz/40 g butter ● 2 oz/ 50 g flour ● butter to grease and flour to dust cake tin
For the chocolate mousse (steps 6 and 7): 3 egg whites ● sugar syrup made with 3½ oz/100 g sugar (see page 194) ● 7 oz/200 g chocolate buttercream (see page 187)
For the kirsch syrup: 2 oz/50 g sugar ● 5 fl oz/150 ml water ● 1½ fl oz/40 ml kirsch
To decorate: milk chocolate flakes

There are many different varieties of chocolate cake in the world. This one, filled with chocolate mousse, is one of the most delicious. It takes some time to prepare, but is not difficult.

1 Beat the eggs and sugar together in a bowl.

2 In another bowl dissolve the cocoa powder in the hot water. Melt the butter and incorporate gradually into the cocoa.

3 Sift the flour into the eggs and sugar, sifting and beating hard alternatively. Add the cocoa mixture from step 2 and stir briefly.

4 Turn the mixture into a buttered and floured 8-in/20-cm cake tin. Place in a preheated oven at 350°F/180°C/mark 4 for 20 minutes.

5 Remove from the oven and cover the tin immediately with a damp cloth to keep the cake soft.

6 Whisk the egg whites until stiff. Cook the sugar syrup to hard-ball stage. Fold the hot sugar syrup carefully into the egg whites and continue to stir until cool.

7 Fold in the chocolate buttercream.

8 Cut the cake into two equal layers. Brush the first layer with the kirsch syrup made with the quantities given above and following the method on page 192. Spread with a layer of chocolate mousse about ¼ in/5 mm thick. Place the second layer of sponge on top and cover the entire cake with the remaining mousse. Place in the refrigerator for 20 minutes for the chocolate mousse to firm. Finally, decorate with the milk chocolate flakes.

Diplomat

2 squares or rectangles puff or flaky pastry (see page 193)   •   1 layer sponge not more than 1½ in/4 cm thick (see page 194)   •   10½ oz/ 300 g rum buttercream (see page 187)   •   Maraschino to soak sponge   •   2 oz/50 g icing sugar

1 Prepare the pastry and sponge.

2 Place a cardboard flan base on a serving dish.

3 Place one of the pastry squares on top of the flan base.

4 Spread a layer of rum buttercream (see page 187) over the pastry.

5 Using a pastry brush, brush the layer of sponge with Maraschino and place on top of the layer of rum buttercream.

6 Spread the sponge with a further layer of rum buttercream.

7 Cover with the second pastry square and dust with icing sugar.

Millefeuille gâteau

4 circles flaky or puff pastry (see page 193)
For the zabaione cream (steps 1-3): 3 egg yolks ● 3½ oz/100 g icing sugar ● 2 fl oz/60 ml dry Marsala ● ½ pt/300 ml double cream
To decorate: 2 sponge fingers, crumbled ● 3½ oz/100 g hazelnuts or almonds, skinned, toasted and finely chopped ● 1 oz/25 g icing sugar ● Chantilly cream (see page 190) ● toasted hazelnuts or almonds or glacé cherries

1 Prepare the zabaione cream: place the egg yolks and icing sugar in a saucepan and beat until light and creamy. Beating continuously, add the Marsala a spoonful at a time.

2 Place the saucepan over a pan of hot water over a gentle heat. Beat until light and airy. Allow to cool.

3 Whip the cream and fold into the egg mixture, stirring from bottom to top.

4 Place a circle of pastry on a serving dish and cover with a layer of zabaione cream.

5 Repeat with the remaining pastry.

6 Cover the top of the gâteau with the remaining zabaione cream.

7 Mix the crumbled sponge fingers with the hazelnuts or almonds and press over the top of the gâteau.

8 Dust with icing sugar.

9 Decorate with rosettes of Chantilly cream. On each rosette place a toasted almond or hazelnut, or a glacé cherry. Store in the refrigerator until ready to serve.

Christmas gâteau

For the almond sponge: 3½ oz/100 g sugar • 6 egg yolks • 6 egg whites • 2 oz/60 g flour • 1 oz/25 g ground almonds • few drops vanilla essence • ½ oz/15 g butter to grease cake tin
For the syrup: 1 oz/25 g sugar • 2-4 tbsp water • 2 fl oz/60 ml Grand Marnier
For the buttercream: 7 oz/200 g butter • 3½ oz/100 g sugar • 3 tbsp water • 2 egg yolks • pistachios, toasted and finely ground • 2 fl oz/60 ml Grand Marnier
To decorate: white, yellow and chocolate marzipan (see page 192) • royal icing and chocolate icing

This gâteau is prepared with an almond sponge, made with the ingredients and quantities given above; follow steps 1-4 of the recipe on page 19. The difference between the plain sponge and the almond sponge lies in the addition of ground almonds to the flour. The decoration of the gâteau can of course be varied to suit any festive occasion.

1 Prepare the almond sponge. Cut a thin layer off the top of the sponge. Cut the remaining sponge into two equal layers and sprinkle the lower layer with Grand Marnier syrup made with the quantities given above and following the method on page 192.

2 Prepare a buttercream with pistachios and Grand Marnier (see page 187), using the ingredients and quantities given above.

3 Place the second layer of sponge on top of the first and cover the entire gâteau with the buttercream.

4 Decorate the top of the cake with a candle made from the white marzipan, with stars made from yellow marzipan and a candlestick made from chocolate marzipan.

5 To ice the cake make two paper icing nozzles or use a piping bag with the finest plain nozzle.

6 Decorate with royal icing (see page 192) and chocolate icing (see page 192).

Trifle with nuts

1 layer sponge about 1 in/2-3 cm thick and 7 in/18 cm in diameter (see page 19, steps 1-4) ● sweet liqueur (such as kirsch, Maraschino, Curaçao) to soak sponge ● confectioner's custard (see page 15, steps 1-3) ● Chantilly cream (see page 190) ● toasted nuts or caramelized dried fruit (see page 190)

1 Place the sponge in a glass dish approximately 9 in/23 cm in diameter.

2 Using a pastry brush, brush the sponge with sweet liqueur of your choice.

3 Spread the sponge with a layer of confectioner's custard ½ in/1 cm thick.

4 Decorate the cake with toasted nuts or caramelized dried fruit.

5 Place the cake in the freezer for at least 30 minutes.

6 Before serving, decorate the top of the cake with Chantilly cream.

26

Sachertorte

5 oz/150 g plain chocolate • 2 tbsp milk • 6 egg whites • 9 oz/250 g sugar • 5 oz/150 g butter • 6 egg yolks • 3½ oz/100 g almonds, skinned, toasted and finely ground • 4 oz/125 g flour • few drops vanilla essence • 2 oz/50 g fine breadcrumbs, or coarse biscuit crumbs • 3-4 tbsp apricot jam • 2 fl oz/60 ml rum to soak sponge • chocolate icing (see page 192) • butter to grease cake tin

1 Melt the chocolate over a low heat with 2 tbsp milk. Whisk the egg whites until stiff.

2 Mix the ingredients together in the following order: cream the sugar with the butter; add the egg yolks, melted chocolate, almonds, whisked egg whites, flour, vanilla essence, breadcrumbs.

3 Pour the mixture into a buttered cake tin and place in a preheated oven at 400°F/200°C/mark 6 for 30 minutes. Remove from the oven and allow to cool for several hours.

4 Cut the cake into three equal layers. Spread the first with apricot jam. Sprinkle the second layer with rum and place on top of the first layer. Spread with apricot jam and cover with the third layer of sponge.

5 Using a palette knife, cover the entire cake with chocolate icing. Leave the icing smooth, or decorate it with more finely piped icing.

Coffee and cream cake

For the cake: 3 eggs • 4 oz/125 g sugar • 3½ oz/100 g flour • 1 oz/25 g butter • 2 tbsp instant coffee • 1 tbsp brandy
For the cream filling: 2 egg yolks • 2 oz/50 g sugar • 1 oz/25 g flour • 5 fl oz/150 ml milk • 1 tbsp icing sugar • 3½ fl oz/100 ml whipped cream • 2 tbsp instant coffee • 2 tbsp brandy
To decorate: ½-¾ pt/300-450 ml Chantilly cream (see page 190) • marzipan (see page 192)

The leaf decoration on this cake is made of marzipan which you can make yourself or buy ready-made. Of course the final decoration is a matter of personal taste. When you have completed the eight steps illustrated opposite, cover the entire cake with Chantilly cream, using a spatula to spread it smoothly. Using a piping bag and, varying the nozzles to achieve different patterns, decorate the cake with the remaining Chantilly cream.

1 Put the eggs and sugar into a basin over a pan of hot water and stir for 8-10 minutes.

2 Sift the flour gradually into the egg and sugar mixture and fold in carefully.

3 Melt the butter; dissolve the coffee in the brandy. Mix the butter and the coffee and brandy solution together and stir into the cake mixture.

4 Line a deep cake tin with buttered greaseproof paper and pour in the cake mixture. Bake in a preheated oven at 325°F/ 170°C/mark 3 for 30 minutes. Leave the cake to cool and then cut into four equal layers.

5 To make the cream filling, beat the egg yolks, add the sugar and then the flour.

6 Warm the milk and add gradually. Transfer the mixture to a pan.

7 Place the pan over a low heat and stir until the mixture thickens. Leave to cool; if necessary place in the freezing compartment of the refrigerator for a few minutes.

8 Stir in the following ingredients in the order given: icing sugar, whipped cream (fold in carefully), the coffee dissolved in the brandy. Spread three layers of the cake with this cream; cover with the fourth layer of cake.

Cassata siciliana

1¾ lb/800 g ricotta or curd cheese • 14 oz/400 g sugar • 2 fl oz/ 60 ml water • ½ tsp powdered cinnamon • 5 oz/150 g plain chocolate, coarsely grated • ¾ lb/350 g candied lemon peel: 7 oz/ 200 g finely diced, 5 oz/150 g cut into large strips • 2 oz/50 g pistachios • 2-4 fl oz/60-125 ml Marsala • 1 lb/500 g sponge (see page 194) • 2-4 fl oz/60-125 ml Maraschino to soak sponge • 7 oz/200 g lemon icing (see page 192) • few drops food colouring (optional) • glacé cherries

'Cassata siciliana' is a cake and not to be confused with the frozen 'Cassata alla siciliana', which is an ice-cream dessert.

1 Beat the ricotta in a bowl until smooth.

2 Heat the sugar in a pan with the water until you have a clear syrup. Pour on to the ricotta, add the cinnamon and mix.

3 Add the chocolate, the finely diced candied lemon peel, the pistachios and the Marsala.

4 Cut the sponge into fingers. Dip in Maraschino and line a shallow glass dish about 10 in/25 cm in diameter with the fingers.

5 Pour the ricotta mixture into the glass dish.

6 Cover with more slices of sponge but do not dip these in liqueur.

7 Place in the refrigerator for at least 4-5 hours.

8 Turn out the cassata on to a cake board, cover the outside with lemon icing tinted with food colouring, if desired, and decorate with the remaining candied peel and with glacé cherries.

Zuccotto

1¾ pt/1 litre double cream ● 3½ oz/100 g icing sugar ● 3 oz/80 g toasted, ground almonds ● 3 oz/80 g toasted, ground hazelnuts ● 2-3 tbsp candied fruit ● 5 oz/150 g plain chocolate, grated ● 1 lb/500 g sponge (see page 194) ● 3 tbsp cognac or brandy ● 3 tbsp rum ● 3 tbsp kirsch ● 1 tbsp Morello cherries ● cocoa powder and icing sugar to decorate

Zuccotto is considered a Tuscan invention; the white and brown decoration is a characteristic feature of this dessert.

1 In a deep bowl whip the cream and fold in the sugar carefully. Add the ground almonds and hazelnuts and candied fruit. Divide the mixture between two bowls. Melt the chocolate, allow it to cool, then fold it into half the cream mixture.

2 Cut the sponge into slices ½-¾ in/1.5 cm thick and sprinkle with the three spirits mixed together. Line a mould or basin with the slices.

3 Pour the plain cream mixture into the mould first.

Place the Morello cherries in the centre. Pour the chocolate-flavoured cream into the mould.

4 Cover the cream with more sponge slices, not dipped in spirit.

5 Chill in the refrigerator for at least 2 hours.

6 Unmould the zuccotto on to a lace doily on a serving dish. Decorate with cocoa powder and icing sugar.

Walnut charlotte

30 sponge fingers (see page 131) • 2 fl oz/60 ml kirsch to soak sponge • 9 oz/250 g butter • 9 oz/250 g icing sugar • 7 oz/200 g ground walnuts • 2 egg yolks • 2 egg whites, whisked • 1 pt/ 600 ml Chantilly cream (see page 190) •
2 oz/50 g glacé cherries • 2 oz/50 g halved walnuts

A charlotte is a dessert of French origin. It is made with sponge fingers or 'boudoir' biscuits, which are dipped in liqueur and used to line the base and sides of a mould; when the dessert is turned out on to a serving dish the sponge fingers form an outer shell for the charlotte cream.
The charlotte mould is similar to the bavarois mould, but without the central funnel. A charlotte may be filled with a bavarois.

1 Line the base and sides of a mould with the sponge fingers dipped in kirsch or the liqueur of your choice.

2 Cream the butter and sugar together. Mix in the ground walnuts, followed by the egg yolks, one at a time, then fold in the beaten egg whites.

3 Pour the walnut cream into the mould and cover

with more sponge fingers dipped in kirsch.

4 Place in the refrigerator for several hours.

5 To serve, unmould the charlotte on to a serving dish and decorate with Chantilly cream, glacé cherries and halved walnuts.

Gâteau St-Honoré

For the base: 1 sponge 10 in/25 cm in diameter (see page 194) ●
Maraschino or sherry to soak sponge
For the choux balls: 18-20 profiteroles (see page 58) ● 1 pt/600 ml
whipped cream or pastry cream (see page 193)
For the caramel: 2 oz/50 g sugar ● 2 tbsp water
For the filling: 7 oz/200 g St-Honoré cream (see page 194) ● 7 oz/
200 g chocolate St-Honoré cream (see page 194)
To decorate: 1 pt/600 ml whipped cream (optional)

This a variation on the classic Gâteau St-Honoré which has a base of sweet shortcrust pastry. St-Honoré was the Bishop of Amiens in north-west France in the 7th century. He is now the patron saint of pastry-cooks.

1 Make the sponge base.

2 Make the profiteroles and use a syringe to fill them with whipped cream or pastry cream.

3 Prepare the caramel syrup following the method on page 194, and brush the tops of the profiteroles with the caramel.

4 Place the sponge on a cake board and sprinkle with Maraschino or sherry.

5 Prepare the St-Honoré cream and use a piping bag to decorate the top of the cake with alternate rows of plain and chocolate St-Honoré cream.

6 Arrange the profiteroles round the edge, separated by whipped cream, if desired.

Strawberry and chestnut tart

For the sweet shortcrust pastry: 5 oz/150 g flour • 2½ oz/70 g butter • 2½ oz/70 g sugar • 1 egg • few drops vanilla essence
For the filling: ½ lb/225 g cooked chestnuts • 3¼ oz/90 g butter • 3¼ oz/90 g sugar • 3½ fl oz/100 ml single cream • 2 egg yolks • 3½ fl oz/100 ml double cream • 1 oz/25 g icing sugar
For the topping: ½ lb/225 g cooked chestnuts • ½ tsp salt • 1½ oz/40 g icing sugar • 1 tbsp kirsch
To decorate: 25-30 strawberries, washed and hulled • 3½ oz/100 g apricot jam

To prepare the chestnuts for use in both the filling and the topping for this tart, cut a slit in the shell of each chestnut. Place the chestnuts in a pan pierced with holes and roast them over a flame until their skins split and come off easily. Remove the shells and skins. Boil the chestnuts in milk to cover, adding 1 tsp of salt to each 1 pt/600 ml milk. When the chestnuts are tender, drain them. If you cannot roast the chestnuts first, you can boil them with their skins on but they will take slightly longer to cook.

1 Make a sweet shortcrust pastry using the quantities given above and following the method described on pages 39-40, steps 1-7. Roll out the pastry to about ¼ in/5 mm thick and line a flan tin.

2 Press the pastry firmly to the sides of the flan tin.

3 Trim away any excess pastry overlapping the edge.

4 Sieve the chestnuts for the filling.

5 Cream the butter and sugar, add the single cream and mix well.

6 Stir in the sieved chestnuts and the egg yolks.

7 Prick the pastry case with a fork, pour the mixture into the pastry case and bake in a preheated oven at 350°F/ 180°C/mark 4 for 15-20 minutes. Allow to cool completely.

8 Whip the double cream and fold in the icing sugar. Spread evenly over the tart. Dip each strawberry in apricot jam and arrange round the edge of the tart. Sieve the chestnuts for the topping, add the salt, sugar and kirsch and mix to a paste. Fill a piping bag with the paste and decorate the flan inside the border of strawberries.

Ricotta cheesecake

For the sweet shortcrust pastry: 10½ oz/300 g flour ● 5 oz/150 g sugar ● 5 oz/150 g butter ● 2 egg yolks ● 1 whole egg
For the filling: 1¼ lb/600 g ricotta or curd cheese ● 10½ oz/300 g caster sugar ● 1 egg ● 3 egg yolks ● 1-2 tsp grated orange rind ● ½ tsp cinnamon ● 2 oz/50 g raisins (optional) ● 2 oz/50 g pine-nuts (optional) ● 1¼ oz/35 g finely chopped candied fruit or peel (optional)
To cover and decorate: meringue made with 5 stiffly beaten egg whites with 9 oz/250 g caster sugar folded in

1 Prepare the sweet shortcrust pastry (see pages 39-40, steps 1-7), using the quantities given above.

2 Roll out to a thickness of ¼ in/5 mm and line a flan tin 10 in/25 cm in diameter. Press the pastry firmly to the bottom and the sides of the flan tin.

3 In a large bowl mix together the ricotta (or curd cheese), sugar, the whole egg and the yolks, the grated orange rind and cinnamon. If you like, add the raisins, pine-nuts and candied fruit.

4 Pour the cheese mixture into the flan tin.

5 Place in a preheated oven at 400°F/200°C/mark 6 for 30 minutes.

6 Make the meringue. About 5 minutes before the tart is cooked remove it from the oven and spread the top with meringue: decorate with more meringue as illustrated, using a piping bag. Return the tart to the oven to finish the cooking and turn the meringue golden.

Quick apple cake

6 apples ● juice of ½ a lemon ● 2 oz/50 g sugar
For the dough: 2 oz/50 g butter ● 4 oz/125 g sugar ● 2 egg yolks ● juice of ½ a lemon ● grated rind of ½ a lemon ● 4 oz/125 g flour ● 1 tsp baking powder ● 3 fl oz/90 ml milk ● 3 tbsp rum ● 3 egg whites ● 1 oz/30 g butter to grease cake tin
To glaze: 1oz/25 g melted butter ● 1 egg yolk
To dust: 3 tbsp icing sugar

1 Peel the apples and use an apple corer or a sharp knife to remove the cores.

2 Sprinkle the apples with lemon juice and sugar and put to one side.

3 Cream the butter and sugar. Beat in the egg yolks, the juice of half a lemon and the grated lemon rind.

4 Sift the flour and baking powder together and add to the mixture together with the milk and rum.

5 Whisk the egg whites and fold them carefully into the mixture, stirring from bottom to top.

6 Pour the mixture into a buttered cake tin or oven-proof dish. Press the apples into the mixture. Brush the cake generously with melted butter and beaten egg yolk.

7 Bake in a preheated oven at 325°F/170°C/mark 3 for 35-40 minutes.

8 Remove from the oven and sprinkle with icing sugar.

Apple pie

For the sweet shortcrust pastry: 7 oz/200 g flour ● 3½ oz/100 g sugar ● ½ tsp salt ● 3½ oz/100 g butter ● 2 egg yolks ● margarine or butter to grease and flour to dust pie dish
For the apple filling: 2 lb/900 g apples ● few drops lemon juice ● 1 large slice lemon ● 4 oz/125 g sugar ● pinch nutmeg ● ½ tsp ground cinnamon ● 2 tbsp flour ● 2 tbsp orange juice
To glaze: 1-2 eggs, beaten

This English recipe dates from the 13th century. For best results, take the butter from the refrigerator a couple of hours before using it; it will be easier to work and will blend more readily with the other ingredients.

1 Peel and core the apples, cut them into large slices and leave in water acidulated with a little lemon juice to prevent discoloration. Place the flour, sugar and salt in a bowl and work in the butter with the fingertips.

2 Add the egg yolks, or a whole egg, and mix in as quickly as possible. Continue to work the pastry on a floured board using a spatula (short pastry should be handled as little as possible, otherwise it loses its soft texture).

3 Roll the pastry out fairly thickly.

4 Lift the pastry frequently on the rolling pin and dust the pastry board with flour so that the pastry does not stick.

5 Fold the pastry into three.

6 Roll the pastry out again fairly thickly.

7 Fold into three again; wrap in cling film or a damp cloth and leave in a cool place to rest for 30 minutes.

8 Roll the pastry out for the last time.

9 Fold in three to form a rectangle, ensuring even thickness all round.

10 Cut the pastry into three pieces, two pieces each two-fifths of the whole and one piece one-fifth.

11 Roll one of the larger pieces of pastry out to a thickness of ¼ in/5 mm.

12 Roll out the second large piece to a thickness of ¼ in/5 mm.

13 Line a buttered, floured pie dish with the first sheet of pastry.

14 Roll out the remaining one-fifth of pastry to a thickness of ¼ in/5 mm. Using a pastry wheel, cut it into strips ½ in/1 cm wide.

15 Drain the apples. Place over a gentle heat with the slice of lemon, sugar, nutmeg, cinnamon, flour and orange juice. Stir occasionally with a wooden spoon.

16 When the apples have softened and turned golden in colour remove from the heat and discard the slice of lemon.

17 Turn the apple filling into the pie dish. Arrange strips of pastry on top of the apple, half in one direction evenly spaced and half across them in the other direction.

18 Brush the pastry strips with beaten egg.

19 Cut a circle from the centre of the second rolled-out piece of pastry and set aside. Use the ring of pastry left to cover the edges of the tart, as illustrated.

20 Trim excess pastry from around the edge.

21 Use a small pastry cutter to cut shapes out of the remaining circle of pastry.

22 Decorate the outer rim of the pie with the shapes spaced at regular intervals. Brush with beaten egg. Score the centre of each decoration. Bake in a preheated oven at 400°F/200°C/mark 6 for 40-45 minutes.

Apple turnover

For the pastry: 9 oz/250 g flour ● ½ tsp salt ● 1 tbsp sugar ●
2 oz/50 g melted butter ● lemon juice ● 1 egg ● milk
For the filling: 2 lb/900 g apples ● 2 oz/50 g almonds ● 2 oz/50 g
pine-nuts ● 2 oz/50 g raisins ● 1 tsp grated orange rind ● 1 tsp
ground cinnamon ● 3½ oz/100 g icing sugar ● 3½ oz/100 g
crumbled biscuits ● 2 tbsp rum or Marsala ● 3½ oz/100 g melted
butter ● 1 tbsp jam (apple jam if possible) ● 1 egg yolk ● butter to
grease and flour to dust tin

1 Work together the flour, salt, sugar, butter, lemon juice and egg. If necessary add a few spoonfuls of milk. Wrap the dough in a cloth and leave to rest in a cool place for 30 minutes.

2 Peel and core the apples and slice very thinly. Add the almonds (coarsely chopped), pine-nuts, raisins, grated orange rind, cinnamon, sugar, crumbled biscuits and the rum and mix.

3 Place the dough on a floured cloth and roll out to ⅛ in/3 mm. Brush the dough with some of the melted butter, then spread with a layer of jam.

4 Spread the filling over half the dough, then carefully fold the other half of the dough over to enclose the filling. Use the cloth to roll the dough over without tearing it.

5 Still holding the turnover in the cloth, transfer to a greased and floured Swiss roll tin. Brush the surface with egg yolk and melted butter. Place in a preheated oven at 350°-375°F/180°-190°C/mark 4-5 for 40-45 minutes, until the surface is golden brown.

Chestnut log

7 oz/200 g tinned chestnuts ● 2-3 tbsp brandy ● 3½ oz/100 g butter ● 7 oz/200 g sugar ● 3 egg yolks ● 5 tbsp milk ● 6 oz/175 g soft breadcrumbs ● few drops vanilla essence ● 2 egg whites ● chocolate-covered chestnuts (see page 190) ● grated chocolate

1 Drain the chestnuts – reserve a few for decoration – and sprinkle with brandy. Leave to stand for 2-3 days or for as long as possible. Cream the butter and sugar together in a bowl.

2 Beat the egg yolks a little and mix into the creamed butter and sugar. Stir in the milk gradually with a wooden spoon.

3 Drain the chestnuts, chop finely and stir into the egg mixture together with the breadcrumbs and vanilla essence.

4 Whisk the egg whites until stiff and fold carefully into the chestnut mixture. Butter a mould, pour the mixture into it and smooth the surface. Cover with buttered foil or greaseproof paper and secure with kitchen string. Steam gently for 40-50 minutes. Unmould and decorate with chocolate-covered chestnuts and grated chocolate.

Lemon meringue pie

For the sweet shortcrust pastry: 7 oz/200 g flour • 3½ oz/100 g caster sugar • ½ tsp salt • 3½ oz/100 g butter • 1 egg
For the lemon filling: 2 oz/50 g flour • 5 oz/150 g icing sugar • 3 egg yolks • 1 tsp grated lemon rind • 3½ fl oz/100 ml lemon juice • 3 egg whites
To spread over lemon filling: peach jelly
For the meringue topping: 3 egg whites • 2¾ oz/75 g icing sugar • 15-20 flaked almonds, toasted

1 Prepare the sweet shortcrust pastry, using the ingredients and quantities given above and following the method described on page 39-40, steps 1-7 (see also page 194). Roll out the pastry and line a flan tin. Prick the pastry all over with a fork and fold the pastry over the edges of the flan tin. To prevent the pastry from rising during baking cover with greaseproof paper weighted with beans or dried peas (these will be removed when the pastry has been baked). Bake the pastry at 400°F/200°C/mark 6 for 10-15 minutes; discard the paper and beans and bake for a further 5-10 minutes.

2 In a bain marie mix the flour, icing sugar, egg yolks, grated lemon rind and juice; beat over low heat until thickened (5-10 minutes). Do not overheat.

3 Remove from the heat. Whisk the egg whites; fold carefully into the lemon mixture, stirring from bottom to top.

4 Pour the filling into the shortcrust pastry base.

5 Brush the surface of the pie with a thin layer of peach jelly.

6 Prepare the meringue topping. Whisk the egg whites and gradually fold in the sugar (1 oz/25 g for each egg white). With a piping bag and star or ribbon nozzle filled with meringue, decorate the pie with diagonal criss-cross lines. Decorate the edges with a thick band of meringue and flaked almonds. Bake in a preheated oven at 400°F/200°C/mark 6 for 5-10 minutes.

Baked cheesecake

For the sweet shortcrust pastry: 7 oz/200 g flour ● 3½ oz/100 g caster sugar ● ½ tsp salt ● 3½ oz/100 g butter ● 1 egg
For the filling: 10½ oz/300 g cream cheese ● 2 eggs ● 1½ oz/40 g melted butter ● 2 oz/50 g flour ● 2 oz/50 g sugar ● few drops vanilla essence ● ½ tsp salt ● 1 tsp grated orange rind ● 3½ fl oz/100 ml whipped cream ● 1 oz/25 g caster sugar
To glaze: 1 egg yolk ● 1 oz/25 g icing sugar ● 1-2 tbsp water

This cheesecake has more or less become the American national dessert; it can be found all over the United States and an annual competition produces thousands of 'Miss Cheesecakes'. Its origins, however, are Roman: in ancient times the Romans made a tart called a 'suavillum', which was made with pastry, cream cheese and honey and which was eaten throughout the Roman Empire.

1 Prepare the sweet shortcrust pastry using the ingredients and quantities given above and following the method described on pages 39-40, steps 1-7. Roll out and use to line a fluted flan tin.

2 Press firmly down over the base and sides of the tin.

3 Prick all over with a fork to prevent the pastry from rising during cooking.

4 Using a wire whisk and a large mixing bowl beat together the cheese, eggs and melted butter to form a cream.

5 Sieve the flour and beat gradually into the mixture; add the sugar, vanilla essence and salt and finally the grated orange rind.

6 In a separate bowl whip the cream and sugar until stiff.

7 Fold carefully into the cheese mixture.

8 Pour the cheese mixture into the flan tin, level the top and glaze with the egg mixture (prepared by dissolving the sugar with the egg yolk and a few spoonfuls of water in a bain marie). Bake in a preheated oven at 400°F/200°C/mark 6 for at least 20 minutes until well browned.

47

Danish bilberry and custard pastry

1-1¼ lb/500-600 g croissant dough (see page 126) ● 7 oz/200 g bilberries
For the custard: 5 fl oz/150 ml milk ● 2 oz/50 g sugar ● ½ oz/15 g flour ● ½ oz/15 g cornflour or potato flour ● 2 egg yolks ● ½ oz/15 g butter
To glaze: 2 egg yolks ● a few tbsp water

1 Prepare the croissant dough following steps 1-7 on page 127.

2 To make the custard, heat the milk and add the sugar, flour and cornflour. Cook, stirring constantly, until it thickens. Remove from the heat and add the egg yolks and butter, stirring hard. Leave to cool.

3 Spread out the dough on a floured surface, and roll out ½ in/1 cm thick. Cut out a square, as illustrated, and remove the excess dough from the centre.

4 Place the dough on an oiled baking tray.

5 Make a depression in the surface of the dough all round the square and spread the custard in the hollow. Cover with the bilberries.

6 Roll out the remaining dough and cut strips ½ in/1 cm wide. Place the strips of dough diagonally across the filling.

7 Leave to rise for at least 1 hour in a warm place. Beat the egg yolks with the water and brush over the whole surface of the pastry.

8 Bake in a preheated oven at 400°F/200°C/mark 6 for 20 minutes.

Chestnut tart

2¼ lb/1 kg chestnut flour • 10 tbsp oil • 1 tbsp sugar • ½ tsp salt • 3½ oz/100 g pine-nuts • 3½ oz/100 g raisins • ½-¾ pt/ 300-450 ml water • 1 sprig rosemary

Chestnut tart or *castagnaccio* is a regional dish from the rural part of northern Tuscany. This tart can be served hot or cold, though its subtle flavour is more fully appreciated when it is eaten hot.

1 In a large bowl mix together the chestnut flour, oil, sugar, salt, three-quarters of the pine-nuts and three-quarters of the raisins. Add enough water to make a soft batter of pouring consistency.

2 Pour the mixture into a large, low-sided flan case which has been brushed with oil: the paste should not be more than ¾-1 in/ 2-2.5 cm thick.

3 Brush the surface with oil. Sprinkle with the remaining pine-nuts, raisins and the rosemary.

4 Cook in a preheated oven at 400°F/200°C/mark 6 for 1 hour.

5 Before serving transfer to a serving dish.

Mont Blanc

1 lb/500 g chestnuts • ½ pt/300 ml milk • 1 tsp salt • 5 oz/150 g sugar • few drops vanilla essence • 2 oz/50 g cocoa powder • 2-3 tbsp rum • knob of butter • 9 fl oz/250 ml Chantilly cream (see page 190)

To decorate (optional): glacé cherries • chocolate strands

This is a French dessert, originated by the famous Parisian chef Escoffier.

1 Make a slit in each chestnut with the point of a knife. Place over a flame in a pan with holes in it (as used by chestnut vendors). Keep the chestnuts moving over the heat for about 5 minutes or until the shells and inner skin can be removed easily.

2 Peel the chestnuts and cook in the milk over a very low heat for approximately 45 minutes until soft. If the mixture becomes too dry add more boiling milk. When soft, drain and press through a food mill.

3 Add the salt, sugar, vanilla essence, cocoa powder, rum and melted butter to the chestnut purée. Pass through the food mill again, catching it on a serving plate in a little heap. Refrigerate for 1 hour.

4 Just before serving cover with Chantilly cream.

5 If liked, the cream can be decorated with glacé cherries and chocolate strands.

Christmas pudding

(makes 2 puddings)

6 oz/175 g shredded suet • 2 oz/50 g flour • 6 oz/175 g fresh white breadcrumbs • ½ lb/225 g raisins • ½ lb/225 g sultanas • 6oz/175 g currants • ½ lb/225 g soft brown sugar • 2 oz/50 g almonds, blanched and chopped • 4 oz/125 g mixed peel, finely chopped • ¼ tsp salt • ¼ tsp ground nutmeg • ¼ tsp ground ginger • ¼ tsp mixed spice • ¼ tsp ground mace • grated rind and juice of ½ a lemon • grated rind and juice of ½ an orange • 2½ fl oz/75 ml brandy and rum mixed • 2½ fl oz/75 ml brown ale • 2 eggs, beaten • butter to grease basins • *For the brandy butter*: 3 oz/80 g butter • 3 oz/80 g caster sugar • 3-4 tbsp brandy

1 Mix together all the dry ingredients in a large bowl, using the hands to blend thoroughly.

2 Mix the fruit juices, brandy and rum and the brown ale with the beaten eggs and add to the dry ingredients. Stir very thoroughly. Cover and leave to stand in a cool place overnight.

3 Stir the mixture and pour into 2 well-buttered pudding basins. Cover each basin with buttered greaseproof paper and foil and secure with string.

4 Place each basin in a large saucepan half filled with boiling water. Cover and steam for 8 hours. Top up with boiling water as necessary.

5 Remove the puddings and leave to cool. Cover with fresh greaseproof paper and foil. Store in a cool place until required.

6 On Christmas Day, steam the pudding for a further 2 hours. Remove the foil and greaseproof paper and turn the pudding out on to a heated serving dish.

7 Pour warmed brandy over the pudding and ignite. Serve with brandy butter, made in the following way: cream together the butter and sugar. Beat in the brandy gradually. Leave to harden in the refrigerator.

Cream wheels with marrons glacés

For the sponge: 2 oz/50 g butter • 2¼ oz/60 g sugar • 3 fl oz/90 ml milk • 2½ oz/70 g flour • few drops vanilla essence • 1 whole egg • 4 egg yolks • 4 egg whites
For the filling: 7 fl oz/200 ml double cream • few drops vanilla essence • ½ oz/15 g icing sugar • 5 marrons glacés, chopped
To brush the roll: 2 fl oz/60 ml rum syrup (see page 192)

This dessert is known by a variety of names because of its shape. Technically speaking the shape is a vortex; the cakes are called 'wheels', 'discs' and various other names besides.

1 Line a rectangular Swiss roll tin with silicon paper or baking parchment.

2 Melt the butter with the sugar over a very low heat.

3 Stir in half the milk and cook together for a few minutes.

4 Add the flour and vanilla essence and mix.

5 Stirring constantly, cook until the dough is thick and no longer sticks to the pan or the spoon. Remove from the heat and allow to cool.

6 Stir in the whole egg and the yolks one by one.

7 Add the remaining milk and mix.

8 Pour the mixture through a sieve to eliminate lumps.

9 Cover the bowl with cling film and allow to rest while you complete the next step.

10 Whisk the egg whites until very stiff.

11 Fold carefully into the egg mixture, stirring from bottom to top.

12 Pour the mixture into the Swiss roll tin and smooth the surface. Bake in a preheated oven at 325°F/170°C/mark 3 for 30 minutes until golden brown.

13 Remove from the oven, allow to cool and remove the paper.

14 Whip the cream and then add the vanilla essence and the icing sugar. Spread over the sponge. Sprinkle the chopped marrons glacés over the cream. Roll very carefully, taking care that none of the filling squeezes out.

15 Wrap the roll in greaseproof paper taking care that the paper touches the outside of the roll only. Leave the roll in a cool place for at least 30 minutes.

16 Remove the paper and brush the roll with the rum syrup. Cut the roll into slices about 1 in/2-3 cm thick.

Pastries and pancakes

Sicilian cream horns

To make about 25 cream horns: 10½ oz/300 g flour ● 1 tbsp sugar ● 1 tsp cocoa powder ● 1 tsp finely ground coffee ● ½ tsp salt ● 2 oz/50 g butter, softened ● 1 egg yolk ● 2-4 fl oz/50-125 ml Marsala ● oil for deep frying
For the filling: 1 lb/500 g ricotta or curd cheese ● 11-12 oz/325-350 g icing sugar ● few drops vanilla essence ● 2 oz/50 g cooking chocolate, grated ● 2 tbsp rum
To decorate: 3½ oz/100 g pistachios, coarsely chopped ● 2 oz/50 g chopped, candied peel ● glacé cherries

1 Mix together the flour, sugar, cocoa powder, coffee and salt.

2 Make a well in the centre, place the softened butter and egg yolk in the centre and work the ingredients to a paste; add enough Marsala to make a dough.

3 Wrap in a cloth and leave to rest in the refrigerator for at least 1 hour.

4 Roll out to ⅛ in/3 mm thick and cut into squares 4 × 4 in/10 × 10 cm. Using the rolling pin, round off two opposite corners of each square. Place each square

of pastry round a plain tin cannoli mould, joining the non-rounded corners of the pastry where they meet.

5 Deep fry in plenty of hot oil until golden and crisp.

6 Remove from the moulds. Mix the ingredients

for the filling and fill the pastry horns when they have cooled completely.

7 Press pistachios and candied fruit into the cream at either end and decorate with glacé cherries.

Profiteroles

For the profiteroles: 9 fl oz/250 ml water ● 3½ oz/100 g butter ● ½ tsp salt ● 1 tbsp sugar ● 5 oz/150 g flour ● 3-4 eggs ● butter to grease and flour to dust baking tray
Cream filling: 3½ oz/100 g sugar ● ½ oz/15 g cornflour or potato flour ● few drops vanilla essence ● 2 fl oz/60 ml milk ● 3 egg yolks ● 9 fl oz/250 ml double cream
To soak profiteroles: 1 tsp Marsala for each profiterole (optional)
To decorate: 2 oz/50 g sugar ● 5 oz/150 g chocolate

'Profiterole' is a French word used to describe the famous dessert of small choux pastry balls filled with cream, coated with chocolate and piled in a pyramid; it can also be applied to small savoury rolls used to garnish certain soups. Having completed the steps illustrated opposite, continue as follows: a) pour a tsp of Marsala over each profiterole; b) using a piping bag and plain nozzle fill each profiterole with the cream made in steps 7 and 8; c) dip each profiterole in chocolate melted with sugar (adjust the quantity of sugar used according to taste); d) arrange the profiteroles in a pyramid on a serving dish and cover with the remaining melted chocolate.

1 Gently heat together the water, butter, salt and sugar until the butter has melted and then bring rapidly to the boil. Turn off the heat and pour in all the flour.

2 Beat vigorously until the flour has been absorbed and the dough forms a ball. Leave to cool slightly.

3 Add the beaten eggs a little at a time, beating vigorously with a wooden spoon each time more beaten egg is added. If the dough is soft enough after the third egg has been added, do not add the fourth. The dough should be shiny and fairly thick.

4 Butter a baking tray and dust with flour. Using a spoon or a piping bag, place small mounds of dough on the baking tray. Bake in a preheated oven at 400°F/200°C/mark 6 for 15-20 minutes.

5 Make the cream filling: mix the sugar, cornflour and vanilla essence with the milk and add this mixture to the egg yolks. Heat gently, stirring until thickened. Allow to cool.

6 Fold the stiffly whipped cream carefully into the above mixture and use to fill the profiteroles.

Brioches with cream and fruit

For the dough: ½ oz/15 g fresh yeast • 9 oz/250 g flour • 6 tbsp lukewarm milk • 3 eggs • 2 oz/50 g sugar • 2 oz/50 g melted butter • ½ tsp salt • butter to grease and flour to dust moulds
To decorate: 16 peach halves or 16 apricots • Chantilly cream (see page 190) • liqueur of your choice (such as Cointreau, Maraschino, kirsch) to soak brioches

The basic recipe for savarins, babas and brioches is the same; they differ only in shape. Babas are made in conical, flat-topped moulds; the savarin in a ring mould and brioches in smooth-sided brioche moulds. The savarin is named after Anthelme Brillat-Savarin, author of *La Physiologie du Goût*, a work full of useful and amusing observations and recipes. This recipe comes from his book and is famous all over the world.

1 Crumble the yeast and mix with 2 oz/50 g flour and the milk. Place the mixture in a bowl, cover and leave in a warm place for 15 minutes until doubled in size.

2 Beat the eggs, add the remaining flour and the yeast mixture and knead for 10 minutes, adding a few spoonfuls of milk if necessary. Leave the dough to rise until doubled in size.

3 Add the sugar to the risen dough, then the melted butter and the salt. Knead until the dough comes cleanly away from the sides of the bowl.

4 Butter the individual brioche moulds, dust with flour and fill two-thirds full with dough. Cover and leave to rise for a third time, until the dough has risen to the top of the mould.

5 Bake for 15-20 minutes in a preheated oven at 325°F/170°C/mark 3.

6 Soak the brioches in liqueur (Cointreau, Maraschino, kirsch) and just before serving decorate with peaches or apricots and Chantilly cream.

Rum babas

For the dough: brioche dough (opposite, steps 1-5) ● butter to grease and flour to dust moulds
For the syrup: 9 fl oz/250 ml water ● 8 tbsp clear honey ● 8 tbsp rum

The rum baba was invented more than two centuries ago by the cook – who was probably French – to King Stanislas of Poland. The dough often contains raisins and after baking, the babas are soaked in rum-flavoured syrup. Sometimes babas are cooked not in conical moulds but in miniature savarin moulds so that their centres can be decorated with fruit and whipped cream.

1 Prepare the dough using the same ingredients and quantities as for the brioches described opposite, but bake the dough in baba moulds.

2 To make the syrup: boil the water and honey together for a few minutes. Add the rum and boil for a few minutes more.

3 Soak the warm babas in the rum syrup either by pouring the syrup over them or immersing them in the syrup. Make small holes all over the babas with a skewer to allow the syrup to penetrate. Serve immediately.

Sweet potato pastries

2 lb/900 g sweet potatoes ● ½ lb/250 g butter ● 5 oz/150 g flour ● 2¼ oz/60 g sugar ● 3 eggs ● 2 oz/50 g butter to grease baking tray
To glaze: 1 egg

1 Cut the sweet potatoes in half lengthwise. Cut out the eyes. Soak the potatoes in a bowl of cold water with a little bicarbonate of soda for 1-2 hours. Drain. Boil the potatoes until tender. Carefully peel away the skins and reserve them.

2 Sieve the potato pulp or mash with a potato masher.

3 Melt a knob of butter in a saucepan over a very low heat. Stir in the sieved sweet potatoes, the flour and sugar. Stir until well blended. Remove from the heat.

4 In a bowl mix the softened butter with the eggs. Add to the mixture in the saucepan, return to a low heat and beat thoroughly until well blended. Remove from the heat and beat in the Marsala.

5 Fill the reserved potato skins with the potato paste.

6 Place on a well-buttered baking tray, brush with beaten egg and bake in a very low oven until golden brown.

Cream doughnuts

For the dough: 14 oz/400 g flour • ½-¾ pt/300-450 ml milk • ¾ oz/20 g fresh yeast • 3 oz/80 g butter • 3 eggs • 2-3 tbsp rum • 2½ oz/70 g sugar • ½ tsp salt • few drops vanilla essence
To fill: pastry cream (see page 193)
To decorate: icing sugar

1 Mix together 2 oz/60 g flour with a little milk and the yeast. Roll the mixture into a ball and set it to rise in warm water until it floats and has doubled in size.

2 Melt the butter; add the eggs and rum. Stir in the remaining flour, sugar, salt and vanilla essence.

3 Add to the ball of yeast and mix well. If necessary add a little milk to make a soft, smooth dough. Set to rise until doubled in volume.

4 Knead the dough on a floured surface for about 15 minutes, until it no longer sticks to the fingers. Roll out to a thickness of ¼-½ in/

5-10 mm. Using a large glass cut circles from the pastry. Sprinkle the circles with flour and leave in a warm place to rise.

5 Deep fry the doughnuts in plenty of hot oil over a moderate heat until they are golden brown.

6 Drain the doughnuts and fill with pastry cream using a piping bag or syringe.

7 Sprinkle with icing sugar just before serving.

Petits fours

For the almond sponge: 9 egg yolks ● 4 oz/125 g sugar ● 3½ oz/100 g ground almonds ● 5 oz/150 g flour ● 7 egg whites
For the filling: ½ lb/225 g apricot jam glaze (see page 192) ● 1 lb/450 g almond paste (see page 187)
For the icing: ¾ lb/350 g fondant icing (see page 192)
To decorate: candied fruits, pistachios or marzipan shapes (see page 192)

1 Prepare the sponge (see page 194) with the ingredients given above.

2 Cover a large, shallow rectangular baking tin with greaseproof paper, oiled on both sides. Pour the sponge mixture into the tin and bake at 400°F/200°C/mark 6 for 15-20 minutes.

3 Remove from the oven, turn out on to a wire rack and peel off the greaseproof paper. Cut off any edges of the sponge that are burnt or over-cooked. Divide the sheet of sponge into two half-sheets.

4 Brush the surface of both halves with apricot jam glaze.

5 Roll out the almond paste between two layers of oiled greaseproof paper until it is the same size as one of the pieces of sponge. Place the almond paste on top of one of the pieces of sponge.

6 Sandwich the two pieces of sponge together, placing the top piece, glazed surface down, over the almond paste. Press gently but firmly together.

7 Cut into small shapes and brush each one with apricot glaze. Cover with fondant icing (tinted with colouring if desired).

8 Before the icing sets decorate with candied fruit, pistachios or marzipan shapes.

Orange crêpes
Raisin crêpes

For the batter: 5 fl oz/150 ml milk • 5 fl oz/150 ml single cream • 6 tbsp Grand Marnier or Cointreau • 4 oz/125 g flour • 2 oz/50 g sugar • ¼ tsp salt • 3 egg yolks • 1 egg white • 1½ oz/40 g butter
For the orange crêpes: 2 oz/50 g butter • 4 oz/125 g sugar • 1 tsp grated orange rind • 1 tbsp cognac • 5 fl oz/150 ml orange juice • slices of orange to decorate
For the raisin crêpes: 5 oz/150 g raisins • 2 tbsp rum • 2 oz/50 g butter • 4 oz/125 g sugar

Crêpes are thin, crisp pancakes which brown in a lacy pattern as they cook. The name comes from the Latin *crispus*, meaning crisp.

Crêpes can be served either as a sweet or a savoury dish. For savoury pancakes the batter is made in the same way, but without the cream, sugar or liqueur.

This basic recipe may be adapted and any number of different kinds of filling substituted.

In crêpes containing grated orange rind an orange liqueur should be used (Grand Marnier or Cointreau); in crêpes containing only orange juice use cognac or brandy; in those containing raisins use rum or a spirit derived from grapes (cognac, brandy, marc, etc.).

1 Pour the milk, cream and orange liqueur (or the liqueur plus the orange juice) into a mixing bowl; sift the flour, sugar and salt into the liquid and mix well — there should be no lumps.

2 Beat the egg yolks and white separately and fold into the mixture.

3 Cover and leave for 1 hour.

4 Melt the butter and add to the mixture.

5 Over a moderate heat warm a frying pan (at least 7 in/18 cm wide) which has been greased with a film of butter or lard. When the pan starts to smoke, pour in just enough batter to cover the base of the pan. Shake the pan to prevent the crêpe from sticking.

6 When the first side is golden, turn the crêpe over to cook the other side. Repeat the operation until all the batter is used.

7 For orange crêpes: beat together the butter, sugar, grated rind and liqueur. Add the orange juice. Cook over a low heat until the mixture thickens. Spread each crêpe with a spoonful of the sauce, roll and arrange on a serving dish. Pour the remaining sauce over the crêpes and decorate with slices of orange.

8 For the raisin crêpes: first soak the raisins in the rum and melt the butter and sugar together in a pan. Add the raisins and spirit. When the sauce thickens, remove from the heat. Spread a spoonful of this sauce on each crêpe, roll and arrange on a serving dish; pour the remaining sauce over the crêpes and serve.

Crêpes Suzette

For the batter: The same ingredients, in the same quantities as in the recipe given on page 66
For the filling: 2 oz/50 g butter • 3 tbsp sugar • juice of 3 oranges • juice of 1 lemon • 1 tsp grated orange rind • 1 tsp grated lemon rind • 4-5 tbsp Grand Marnier
To flame the crêpes: 4 tbsp cognac

Tradition has it that these crêpes were first given the name Suzette by Edward VII of England; the King was taken with the beauty of one of his guests named Suzette, just at the moment when, by mistake, his French chef Henri Carpentier had allowed the liqueur in the pan to ignite. As if nothing were amiss the chef served the flaming pancakes.

The following variations of the basic crêpe recipe are suggested: *lemon pancakes* (with lemon juice and sugar); *chocolate pancakes* (with melted chocolate); *ice-cream pancakes* (with vanilla ice-cream, orange juice, sugar and Calvados); *crêpes à l'impériale*, (with redcurrant jelly, crumbled macaroons and pineapple) and *crêpes flambées au Grand Marnier*.

1 Prepare the batter following the method described on page 67.

2 Melt the butter and sugar in a frying pan over a low heat, then add the juices and grated rind of the orange and lemon. Allow the liquid to evaporate slightly so that the sauce thickens, then add the liqueur and stir.

3 Fry the crêpes and immerse them one by one in this sauce, then arrange them, folded in quarters, on a serving dish. Serve immediately.

4 If desired, heat the cognac, sprinkle it over the crêpes and ignite. Serve immediately.

Bulgarian apples

For each serving: 1 small sweet shortcrust pastry flan base (see page 39-40, steps 1-7) ● 1 large apple ● 3½ fl oz/100 ml water ● 7 fl oz/200 ml red wine ● 1 tbsp sugar ● 1 tbsp yogurt ● 3 tbsp confectioner's custard (see page 190)
For the filling: (optional) 5 fl oz/150 ml milk ● few drops vanilla essence ● 1 tsp potato flour or cornflour ● 2 tbsp redcurrants or 1 tbsp redcurrant jelly ● 1 tbsp chopped almonds and toasted, chopped hazelnuts
To decorate: (optional) few clusters black grapes, glazed

There are hundreds of different ways of cooking apples; they are often baked in the oven and are usually cooked with sugar and occasionally with wine or a liqueur such as Calvados. Among the best known recipes are: *apples Frédéric* (with lemon cream, sponge cake and Maraschino); *apples Joséphine* (a French recipe using rice and raspberry syrup); *apples parisiennes* (with various fruits in syrup, chopped almonds and Calvados); *Spanish apples* (with fruit in syrup, chopped almonds, dried figs, glacé cherries and honey); *baked apples with bilberries*; *apples cardinal* (with vanilla cream, fruit in syrup, hazelnuts, orange juice, Curaçao and topped with red cherries to resemble a cardinal's hat, hence the name).

1 Prepare the flan base. Peel the apple and remove the core with an apple corer or sharp knife.

2 Cook the apple in the water, wine and sugar until tender; drain. Reserve the cooking liquid.

3 Mix the yogurt and the custard and spread a layer about ½ in/1 cm thick on the flan base.

4 Place the apple on top.

5 If desired, fill the centre of the apple with the vanilla and redcurrant mixture prepared in the following way: reduce the cooking liquid from the apple with the milk, vanilla essence, potato flour and redcurrants or jelly. Mix the paste with the chopped almonds and the toasted, roughly chopped hazelnuts.

6 If desired, decorate with a few clusters of glazed black grapes (see page 79).

Cream puffs

For the choux pastry: 9 fl oz/250 ml water ● 3½ oz/100 g butter ● 1 tbsp sugar ● ½ tsp salt ● 5 oz/150 g flour ● few drops vanilla essence or 1 tsp grated lemon rind ● 3-4 eggs ● butter to grease and flour to dust baking tray
For the filling: Chantilly cream (*see* page 190) or pastry cream (*see* page 193)

Choux pastry is used for making profiteroles and chocolate eclairs; it can also be used for savoury dishes (in which case salt or spices or cheese are added to the pastry instead of sugar). The filling can be mixed with chopped fresh or candied fruit.

1 Put the water, butter, sugar and salt in a saucepan with high sides and bring to the boil over a moderate heat. Turn off the heat as soon as boiling point is reached.

2 Sieve the flour into this mixture.

3 Over a moderate heat stir vigorously with a wooden spoon until the mixture thickens and begins to sizzle. Remove from the heat and allow to cool, stirring continuously.

4 Add the vanilla essence or the grated lemon rind. Add the eggs one by one, beating each egg a little first and adding it to the mixture gradually.

5 The paste should not be too soft; if it is, it means that the liquid was not reduced enough in step 3. To avoid too soft a mixture add the eggs one at a time, and do not add the fourth egg unless necessary.

6 Butter a baking tray and dust with flour.

7 Place the paste in little heaps on the baking tray using a piping bag or a spoon. Bake in a preheated oven at 400°F/200°C/mark 6 for about 20 minutes. Allow to cool.

8 Prepare the Chantilly cream or the pastry cream and use a piping bag to fill the puffs with cream. Decorate with more cream, if desired.

Fruit tartlets

For the pastry: 3½ oz/100 g butter ● 3½ oz/100 g sugar ● 2 egg yolks or 1 egg ● 7 oz/200 g flour ● ½ tsp salt ● grated lemon rind or vanilla essence
For the filling: 8 tbsp apricot jam ● 15 tbsp custard (see page 48, step 2) ● fresh or tinned fruit
For the almond cream filling: 3½ oz/100 g butter ● 3 oz/80 g icing sugar ● 3 egg yolks or 1 egg ● 2 tbsp rum ● 3½ oz/100 g ground almonds
To brush over the filling: kirsch syrup (see page 192) ● apricot jam glaze (see page 192) ● few tsp kirsch

These fruit tartlets are well known and popular the world over. This recipe is the classic method of preparation which, though elaborate, is not difficult. The tartlets can be cut into a variety of shapes and can be made smaller or larger, with a sweet shortcrust pastry base and a fruit filling and glaze of your choice.

1 Prepare the pastry: work the softened butter (take it from the refrigerator a couple of hours before you start work) to a cream.

2 Add the sugar and beat well.

3 Beat in the yolks (or whole egg) gradually.

4 Add the flour, salt and grated lemon rind or vanilla essence and mix well.

5 Cover and leave to rest.

6 Knead the dough on a floured surface for 1 minute.

7 Flatten the dough with the palm of your hand.

8 Roll out the dough.

9 Shape the dough into a rectangle.

10 Roll out to a thickness of ¼ in/5 mm.

11 Cut out circles ¾ in/ 2 cm larger than the tins (which should be about 1½ in/4 cm in diameter).

12 Place a circle of pastry in each tin, pressing it firmly against the sides.

13 Trim the extra pastry from the edge of the tin.

14 Place ½ tsp apricot jam over the base of each tart.

15 Beat the butter to a cream in a mixing bowl; beat in the icing sugar and the egg yolks; add the rum, a few drops at a time.

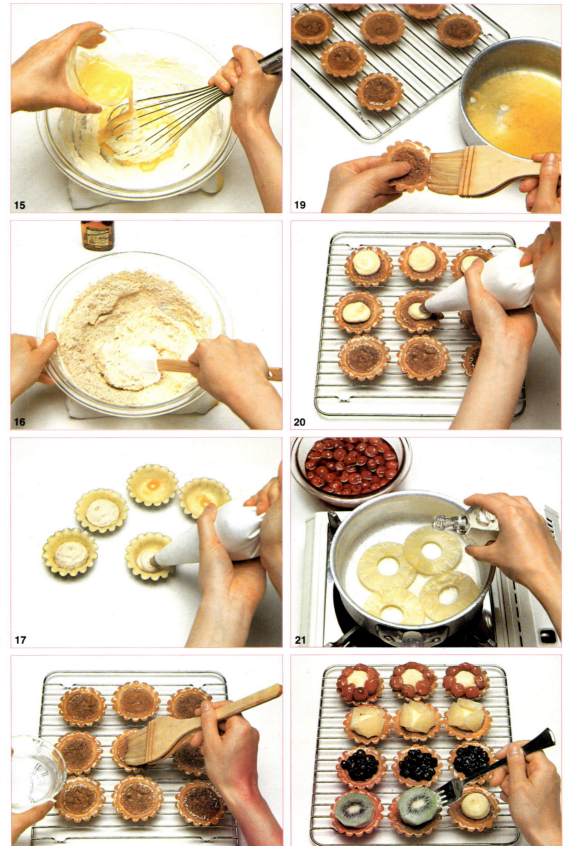

16 Stir in the ground almonds.

17 Use a piping bag to fill each tartlet with the almond cream. Bake in a preheated oven at 350°F/180°C/mark 4 for 15 minutes. Remove from the oven and allow to cool. Take the tartlets out of the tins.

18 Brush generously with kirsch syrup, so that the almond cream absorbs the syrup.

19 Brush each tartlet with apricot jam glaze.

20 Using a piping bag with plain nozzle pipe a tbsp of custard on to each tartlet.

21 Sprinkle the fruit with kirsch.

22 Fill each tartlet with fruit.

Nuns' chatter

For the dough: 10½ oz/300 g flour ● 3½ oz/100 g sugar ● ½ tsp salt ● few drops vanilla essence ● 1 tsp grated lemon or orange rind ● 2 oz/50 g butter ● 3 egg yolks ● 1 egg white ● 2 fl oz/60 ml Marsala or liqueur ● 2-4 tbsp orange juice ● few tbsp milk
To dust: icing sugar ● oil, lard or margarine for deep frying

The Italian name for these fried sweetmeats (and perhaps their original name) is 'nuns' ribbons': this name is now lost in a mass of regional names. In Lombardy the 'ribbons' have become 'chiacchiere' which means 'chatter', and this is now the most frequently used name, more common than any of the other regional terms. 'Chiacchiere' are a Carnival sweetmeat made all over Italy, often with slight variations.

1 Mix together the flour, sugar, salt, vanilla essence, grated lemon or orange rind, softened butter, egg yolks and white, liqueur and orange juice. Add a few spoonfuls of milk if necessary. The dough should be firm enough to roll out thinly with a rolling pin. Roll out, then, using a pastry wheel, cut ribbons 1½-2 in/4-5 cm wide.

2 Twist each ribbon carefully; deep fry in hot oil until lightly browned.

3 Drain well and sprinkle with icing sugar.

Fruit desserts

Glazed fresh fruit

one or more types of fresh fruit ● glacé icing (see page 192) or liqueur glacé icing (see page 192)

Choose your liqueur according to the fruit you are using. For example, use grappa, cognac or brandy with grapes and kirsch, cherry brandy or Maraschino with cherries.

1 Wash the fruit and dry carefully with a clean cloth.

2 Dip the fruit into the glaze and allow the glaze to harden.

Peaches in kirsch

For the cake: 2 oz/50 g butter ● 3½ oz/100 g flour ● 4 oz/125 g
icing sugar ● 4 eggs ● 2 oz/50 g cornflour or potato flour ● few
drops vanilla essence ● kirsch or Cointreau to soak sponge
For the frangipane cream: 2 egg yolks ● 2 oz/50 g sugar ● 4 tbsp
flour ● 4 tbsp ground almonds ● 5 fl oz/150 ml milk ● few drops
vanilla essence ● *For the cream*: 7 oz/200 g icing sugar ● 1-2 tbsp
kirsch ● 4 egg whites ● 2 oz/50 g ground almonds ● 7 fl oz/
200 g Chantilly cream (see page 190) ● *To decorate*: about 20 fresh
or tinned peach slices ● 2-3 tbsp caramel (see page 163, step 1)

1 This cake is usually
cooked in a paper case, as
illustrated. The case can also
be made of foil, or can be
bought ready made.

2 Melt the butter in a bain
marie and then leave to
cool.

3 Sieve the flour.

4 Mix together the eggs
and sugar in a bain marie.

5 Remove from the heat
and beat vigorously.

6 Using a balloon whisk,

continue to beat until the
mixture is thick and similar
in colour and consistency to
whipped egg whites.

7 Fold in the flour, stirring
from bottom to top,
followed by the cornflour
and the vanilla essence.

8 Stir in the cooled melted butter.

9 Pour the mixture into the paper case (or into a foil case buttered and dusted with flour). Bake in a preheated oven at 325°F/170°C/mark 3 for 45 minutes.

10 The cake is cooked when a toothpick or skewer inserted into it comes out clean. Remove from the oven.

11 Turn upside-down and allow to cool. Prepare the frangipane cream in the following way (steps 12-16):

12 Beat together the egg yolks and sugar until the mixture is pale and smooth.

13 Fold in the flour and the ground almonds, which should be lightly toasted.

14 Add the milk and the vanilla essence.

15 Pour the mixture through a sieve to eliminate lumps.

16 Stir constantly over a

15

19

16

20

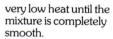

17

21

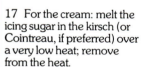

18

22

very low heat until the mixture is completely smooth.

17 For the cream: melt the icing sugar in the kirsch (or Cointreau, if preferred) over a very low heat; remove from the heat.

18 Whisk the egg whites and fold into the melted sugar. Carefully fold in the ground almonds and then the Chantilly cream.

19 Brush the cake generously all over with kirsch or Cointreau.

20 Spread a layer of frangipane cream about ½ in/1 cm thick over the cake.

21 Arrange the peaches in slices on top of the frangipane cream. Using a piping bag pipe the cream (made as illustrated in steps 17 and 18) around the fruit.

22 Decorate the peaches with caramel using a piping bag and very fine nozzle. Just before serving, sprinkle more kirsch or Cointreau over the peaches.

Almond-filled dried fruit and nuts

a variety of dried fruits and nuts: dates, prunes, walnuts, almond paste (see page 187) • food colouring (optional) • melted chocolate (optional)

1 Remove the stones from the dates and prunes, cutting the fruit in half or leaving the two halves slightly joined. Fill with the almond paste.

2 For the walnuts, divide the kernel in half and sandwich the two halves together with the almond paste (plain or coloured with food colouring). You can also dip stuffed dried fruit and nuts into melted chocolate and allow the chocolate to harden.

Baked apple

For each serving: 1 apple • knob of butter • 1 tbsp jam • 1 crumbled biscuit • flaked almonds • 1 tsp caster sugar • 2 fl oz/60 ml Marsala or port

1 Wash and dry the apple. Remove the core. With a sharp knife cut a circle right round the apple. Place in a buttered baking dish.

2 Mix the jam with the crumbled biscuit and stir until smooth; fill the centre of the apple with this mixture.

3 Dot the top of the apple with butter and with flaked almonds.

4 Sprinkle the apple with the sugar; this will form a crust when the apple is cooked.

5 Pour the Marsala or port into the baking dish and bake the apple in the top part of the oven, preheated to 350°F/180°C/mark 4 for 30 minutes.

Pears in white wine

3 large pears • 2 oz/50 g sugar • 5 fl oz/150 ml dry white wine •
5 fl oz/150 ml water • piece of lemon peel • 2 cloves

1 Peel the pears, cut them in half and remove the cores.

2 Place the pears in a pan with the remaining ingredients (reserving half the wine) over a moderate heat.

3 Simmer until the pears are tender.

4 Drain the pears and place on a serving dish.

5 Add the remaining wine to the cooking liquid. Bring to the boil, lower the heat and simmer for 5-10 minutes.

6 Remove the cloves and lemon peel. Pour the syrup over the pears and allow to cool before serving.

Fruit salad and cream

2 lb/900 g fresh or tinned fruit (apples, pears, strawberries, oranges, peaches, apricots, cherries, pineapple, bilberries, raspberries, and so on) ● 3½ oz/100 g sugar ● few drops vanilla essence ● juice of 1 lemon ● 2-3 tbsp rum or Maraschino ● 18 fl oz/500 ml single cream ● 2 oz/50 g chopped nuts

1 Wash, drain and peel the fresh fruit. Slice the fresh and the tinned fruit.

2 Place in a large serving bowl.

3 Mix together the following ingredients: the sugar, vanilla essence, lemon juice, liqueur. Pour over the fruit salad and stir.

4 Pour over the cream and scatter the chopped nuts on top.

5 Leave to stand in a cool place for several hours before serving.

Turkish oranges

6 juicy oranges • ¾ lb/350 g caster sugar • 7 fl oz/200 ml water • 2 cloves

1 Peel the oranges thinly, taking care not to cut away the pith with the rind. Cut the peel into very thin strips.

2 Cover the peel with cold water, bring to the boil and drain when the rind is tender.

3 Place the sugar, 3½ fl oz/ 100 ml of water and the cloves in a saucepan and heat gently until the mixture begins to caramelize.

4 Add the shredded peel and 3½ fl oz/100 ml water and stir until the peel is coated with syrup. Leave to cool slightly.

5 Carefully spoon the syrup and caramelized peel over the oranges, turning them so that they are evenly covered with syrup and rind.

6 Chill the oranges in the refrigerator for several hours. Before serving, quarter the oranges from top to bottom.

Peach Melba

10½ oz/300 g raspberries (or redcurrants, or a jar of raspberry or redcurrant jam) • 4 tbsp warm water • 5oz/150 g icing sugar • 3-4 tbsp lemon juice • few drops vanilla essence • 2-3 tbsp raspberry liqueur (or any sweet liqueur) • 1½ lb/700 g vanilla ice-cream (see page 182 or use ready-made) • 12 peach halves (tinned or fresh; in the latter case, peel and stone the peaches)

This recipe was created nearly a century ago by the celebrated French chef Auguste Escoffier in honour of the famous Australian soprano, Nellie Melba. The most important gastronomic innovations of the last century seem for the most part to have been linked to the world of opera, either to singers like Melba or to composers like Rossini and Bellini.

1 Purée the raspberries with the water in a blender. If you are using jam, heat it gently with a little water.

2 In a large bowl mix together the raspberry purée, sugar, lemon juice, vanilla essence and liqueur. Place in the refrigerator for 1 hour.

3 Place a layer of ice-cream in the bottom of 6 glasses or dishes; place 2 peach halves on the ice-cream. (If the peaches are fresh they should be prepared in the following way: boil 18 fl oz/ 500 ml water with 6 oz/ 175 g sugar and simmer the peaches in this syrup for not more than 5 minutes.) Add 2 scoops of ice-cream and pour over the purée.

4 Serve at once; or place in the refrigerator until required.

Hawaiian fruit salad

½ a pineapple • 2 bananas • juice of ½ a lemon • 2 kiwi fruit • 1 mango • 3-4 lettuce leaves • 2 mandarin oranges • 10 tinned cherries • 2 tbsp sugar
For the orange cream: 3½ fl oz/100 ml orange juice • 2 oz/50 g sugar • 1 egg yolk • 7 fl oz/200 ml double cream

This is a rather special fruit salad, served with an unusual orange cream. Fruit salads are usually topped with single or whipped cream, or with a sweet liqueur, such as Marsala, Maraschino or kirsch. Some more elaborate fruit salads are garnished with yogurt, cream cheese, chopped toasted or pralined nuts, or whole nuts such as pine-nuts. This Hawaiian fruit salad should be chilled for at least 2 hours before serving.

1 Drain off the juice from the pineapple half.

2 Remove the hard core from the half pineapple. Cut all round the flesh of the pineapple so that it can be removed in chunks with a teaspoon.

3 Lay the empty pineapple half cut side down on a cloth to drain the fruit of the remaining juice.

4 Peel and slice the bananas and sprinkle with the lemon juice.

5 Peel and slice the kiwi fruit.

6 Peel the mango, remove the stone and cut the fruit into pieces.

7 Arrange the lettuce leaves in the pineapple half and fill with the drained fruit pieces; add the mandarins in segments and the cherries. Sprinkle with sugar.

8 To make the orange cream, place the orange juice in a pan, add the sugar and dissolve over a low heat. Remove from the heat. Beat the egg yolk in a basin with a metal whisk and add to the orange mixture. Stir over a very low heat until the custard thickens. Allow to cool completely. Whip the cream and stir into the orange sauce. Chill the cream in the refrigerator and pour over the fruit salad just before serving.

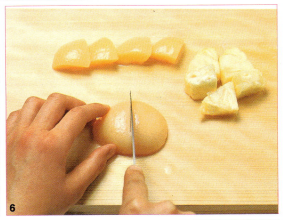

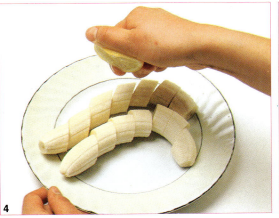

Melon Portuguese

1 melon weighing about 2 lb/900 g ● 2 oz/50 g sugar ● ½ tsp cinnamon ● 7 fl oz/200 ml white port
For the Chantilly cream: 7 fl oz/200 ml double cream ● 1 tbsp sugar

This fruit salad is served in the shell of the melon and can be prepared in a number of different ways: you can add bilberries and sprinkle the top with pistachios, use kirsch or Maraschino instead of port, or mixed fruit salad instead of melon on its own. Try adding vanilla ice-cream and brandy to the mixed fruit, or kirsch to a salad of pineapple and bananas.

1 With the stalk uppermost, cut a zig-zag round the melon and remove the top. Scoop out the seeds.

2 Remove the flesh from the melon using a melon scoop.

3 Replace the balls of melon in the shell; add

sugar and cinnamon and leave to stand for 15 minutes.

4 Add the port and place in the refrigerator for 1 hour.

5 Serve in small glass dishes and decorate with Chantilly cream (see page 190).

Exotic desserts

Manjyu

For the filling: 9 oz/250 g red aduki beans ● 6 oz/175 g sugar ● ½ tsp salt
For the covering: 3 oz/80 g rice flour ● 2¼ oz/60 g Japanese yam (yamanoimo) or sweet potato ● 4 oz/125 g sugar
To decorate: few drops sour cherry syrup

1 Soak the beans in cold water for 1 hour. Boil the aduki beans in water to cover over a moderate heat for 45-60 minutes; add more water if necessary and skim the surface of the water every so often.

2 Drain the beans, return to the pan over heat and add the sugar. Stir while the sugar dissolves and moisture disappears.

3 Remove from the heat, add the salt and allow to cool.

4 Form 20 small balls, dusting the hands with a little rice flour so that the mixture does not stick.

5 Grate the yam and then reduce to a pulp using a pestle and mortar. Mix in the rice flour and sugar and a little water if necessary.

6 Make 20 balls and flatten them into flat circles between the palms of the hands.

7 Place a ball of the bean filling in the centre of each flat circle. Lift the edges of the circle to enclose the ball.

8 Place a damp cloth in the bottom of a steamer. Arrange the sweets, join side down, on the cloth.

9 Put the steamer over a pan of boiling water and steam rapidly for 8 minutes.

10 Cool the sweets using a fan. The more air fanned over the sweets, the glossier the surface of the sweets will be.

11 Before serving, pour a drop of sour cherry syrup on to each sweet.

Japanese 'oranges'

5 oz/150 g red aduki beans ● 9 oz/250 g sugar ● ½ tsp salt ●
7 oz/200 g rice
To cover: 2 tbsp soya bean flour mixed with 2 tbsp sugar and a pinch
of salt ● 4 tbsp sesame seeds, toasted and coarsely chopped, mixed
with 2 tbsp sugar and a pinch of salt

In ancient times this dessert was known by two different names depending on the season of the year. In spring it was called *botamochi*, from the Japanese name for the peony. In autumn it was called *ohaghi*, from a plant called *haghi*. Today it is traditionally eaten during *higan*, a Buddhist religious festival.

1 Pour in sufficient water to cover the aduki beans and boil for 45-60 minutes.

2 While the beans are cooking skim the surface of the water every now and then. Top up with more boiling water if necessary.

3 Drain the beans. Return them to the pan, add the sugar and mix well. Heat gently, stirring carefully until reduced. Add the salt.

4 Transfer to a large dish and allow to cool.

5 Boil the rice in salted water for 12-15 minutes or until well cooked. Drain well and allow to rest for a few minutes, then pound with a wooden pestle or rolling pin.

6 Make 20 small balls with the rice and divide the aduki paste into 20 portions. Spread a damp cloth over the palm of your left hand, place a portion of aduki paste on the cloth and flatten slightly. Place a ball of rice in the middle then wrap the cloth round both with your hand and squeeze into a ball. Leave one-third of the *ohaghi* plain; cover one-third with soya bean flour and the remaining third with the sesame seed mixture.

Sweet potato balls

7 oz/200 g sweet potatoes ● 3 oz/80 g sugar ● ½ tsp salt ● 1 tsp green tea powder ● 4 chestnuts, cooked and peeled (see page 190) or 4 marrons glacés

The Japanese sweets illustrated here may be moulded in various ways. You can make them whichever shape you prefer. Cook fresh chestnuts or use marrons glacés, then halve each chestnut or marron.

1 Wash, peel and cut the sweet potatoes into slices ½-¾ in/1.5 cm thick. Soak them in water for half an hour so that they lose their bitter flavour.

2 Cover with water and boil them until tender (when a toothpick or skewer goes through them easily).

3 Drain and sieve while still warm. Use a wooden spatula to press them through the sieve.

4 Place the pulp in a saucepan with the sugar and bring to the boil, stirring constantly. Add the salt, mix and remove from the heat. Allow to cool.

5 Make 9 equal balls. Mix one ball with the tea powder (softened in a few drops of water if necessary). Spread a damp cloth over the palm of your left hand, place one of the 8 balls in your hand and add one-eighth of the green ball.

6 Flatten the ball, using the edge of the cloth, and form a flat circle 4 in/10 cm in diameter. The green part should be on the outside of the circle.

7 Place half a chestnut in the centre of each circle (or a whole chestnut if they are small).

8 Using the cloth, close the circle around the chestnut and shape into a firm ball. Repeat steps 5 to 8 for the other 7 balls of paste.

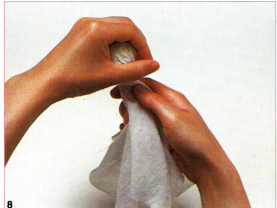

Misuyokan

¾ lb/350 g aduki beans ● 11¼ oz/310 g sugar ● ½ tsp salt ● 1 stick tengusa gelatine ● 1 pint/600 ml water

This is a typical Japanese summer sweet. *Tengusa* is a kind of seaweed. The gelatine obtained from it is called *kanten* and can be found in specialist oriental food shops.

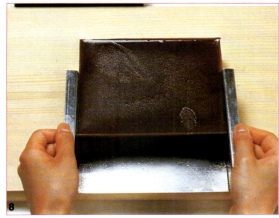

1 Cook the aduki beans as described in steps 1 and 2 on page 96. Mash the beans through a sieve with a wooden pestle. Discard the skins left in the sieve.

2 Place the puréed beans in a muslin cloth and squeeze hard to remove excess water. The bean paste remains in the cloth.

3 Place the bean paste in a saucepan over a very low heat. Pour in 9 oz/250 g sugar, stir until the paste has thickened and then add the salt.

4 Soak the *kanten* (tengusa gelatine) in water for 30 minutes. Wrap it in a cloth and squeeze. Dissolve completely in 1 pint/600 ml water in a pan over medium heat.

5 Add the remaining sugar and allow to dissolve. Remove from the heat and strain through a cloth placed over a metal sieve.

6 Return to the heat and add the bean paste gradually, stirring constantly. When the mixture begins to boil, lower the heat and cook for a further 2-3 minutes. Add more salt to taste if necessary.

7 Remove from the heat and cool quickly by placing the pan in cold water; stir constantly.

8 Turn into a dampened mould. Allow to set in a cool place. Turn out and cut into blocks.

Dango

(Sweets for the Mitarashi festival)

For the dough: 9 oz/250 g rice flour ● 5 fl oz/150 ml tepid water
For the sauce: 3 tbsp sugar ● 3 tbsp water ● 3 tbsp soy sauce ●
1 heaped tbsp potato flour or cornflour

Mitarashi is a Tokyo festival. The soy sauce in which these *dango* are served has always been a great favourite with Japanese children. The sweets are even more delicious if they are allowed to burn slightly during cooking.

1 Make a dough with the rice flour and tepid water.

2 Spread a damp cloth over the base of a steamer. Break the dough roughly into large pieces by hand and place on the cloth. Steam over fast boiling water for 20-30 minutes.

3 As soon as the pieces of dough are cooked pound them with a wooden pestle. Divide the resulting paste into two; roll the two pieces into long sausages ¾ in/2 cm in diameter.

4 Place in iced water for a few minutes to harden. Dry with a cloth, cut into ¾ in/ 2 cm lengths and roll each length by hand into a ball.

5 Wet skewers and thread 4-5 balls on to each one.

6 Place the sauce ingredients in a pan and heat gently until thickened.

7 Grill the balls until they begin to burn.

8 Place the balls on a serving dish and cover with the sauce.

Warabi mochi

2 oz/50 g rice flour ● 3½ oz/100 g warabi flour ● 7 oz/200 g icing sugar ● ½ pt/300 ml water
To sprinkle over: soya bean flour (*kinako*) ● sugar to taste

Warabi is the Japanese term for the plant *pteridium aquilinium*, a kind of fern. Warabi flour is available from specialist oriental stores. *Mochi* is the name of a certain type of rice. This dessert is particularly popular in summer.

1 Mix the two types of flour and sugar with water in a pan, sieving the flour gradually into the water to avoid lumps.

2 Heat gently and stir constantly until transparent.

3 Place in a mould, allow to cool, then place in the refrigerator.

4 Unmould and cut into squares.

5 Prepare the mixture of soya bean flour and sugar and spinkle over the cubes just before serving.

Candied sweet potatoes

14 oz/400 g sweet potatoes • 1 lb/450 g sugar • 5 fl oz/150 ml water • sugar crystals

1 Wash the sweet potatoes and, without peeling them, cut into slices about ½ in/ 1 cm thick. Leave to soak in water for about 1 hour.

2 Boil the potatoes, but do not allow to become too soft. Rinse in cold water, allow to cool and drain well.

3 Melt 10½ oz/300 g of the sugar in a pan with 5 fl oz/ 150 ml water.

4 Add the slices of potato. Remove from the heat as soon as boiling point is reached and leave to stand for 5 hours.

5 Return to the heat and remove again just as boiling point is reached.

6 Remove the potatoes from this syrup; add 3½ oz/ 100 g sugar to the syrup and, when the sugar has dissolved, add the potatoes. Remove from the heat as soon as boiling point is reached. Leave to stand for 3 hours.

7 Repeat step 6 again, adding the last 2 oz/50 g sugar and leaving the potatoes to stand for 1 hour.

8 Allow to cool completely, then drain; scatter with sugar crystals and serve.

Wheel of happiness

(Water melon and lychees with lemon jelly)

1 stick agar-agar or ½ oz/15 g gelatine ● 12 fl oz/350 ml water ● ½ lb/225 g sugar ● juice of 1 lemon ● 1 small water melon ● 1 tin lychees

1 Soak the agar-agar in water for at least 1 hour, changing the water from time to time. If using gelatine, soften it in a little hot water and add it to the pan.

2 Squeeze the agar-agar to remove excess water. Place in a pan with the 12 fl oz/350 ml water and heat until completely dissolved.

3 Add the sugar, allow to dissolve completely then remove from the heat. Add the lemon juice and stir.

4 Strain through a cloth and allow to cool.

5 Remove the seeds from the water melon and scoop out the flesh with a melon-baller. Drain the lychees. If using fresh lychees (which

are sometimes available in fruit shops) remove the skin and stones.

6 Dip the fruit into the liquid from step 4 several times and place in the refrigerator so that the jelly sets around the fruit.

7 Rinse an 8-in/20-cm ring mould with cold water, then fill with the remaining

hot jelly mixture from step 4. Leave to stand until cool and then place in the refrigerator.

8 Unmould the jelly onto a serving dish. (The dish in the photograph is called the 'Wheel of Happiness' in China.) Surround with the jellied fruit balls before serving.

105

Chi-ma-chu

(Sesame seed balls)

3½ oz/100 g red soya bean flour • 7 fl oz/200 ml water • 1 lb/
450 g sugar • 2 tbsp lard • 5 oz/150 g rice flour • 3½ oz/100 g
plain flour • 5 fl oz/150 ml water • 2½ oz/70 g white sesame
seeds • oil for deep frying

In China these fried sesame sweetmeats are offerd to
guests during certain festivals; at the time of the
Chinese New Year they are supposed to bring good
luck.

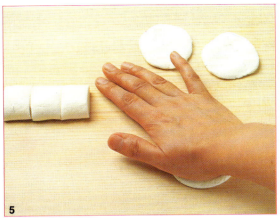

1 Place the red soya flour and the water in a pan and mix with a wooden spoon over a moderate heat. Add the sugar and stir until a fairly firm paste is formed. Remove from the heat and allow to cool.

2 Melt the lard in a clean pan; add the cooled paste and cook over a low heat, stirring with a wooden spoon.

3 Mix the rice flour and the plain flour together and add 5 fl oz/150 ml water gradually. Work into a pliable dough.

4 Sprinkle the work top with rice flour and roll the dough into a long cylinder, 1¼ in /3 cm in diameter.

5 Cut the roll into 30 pieces 1 in/2.5 cm long. Flatten each piece with the palm of the hand to make small circles.

6 Using the cooled red soya paste from step 2 make small balls ½ in/1.5 cm in diameter. Enclose in the circles of dough and roll between the hands to form smooth balls.

7 Put the sesame seeds in a shallow tray and roll the balls in them, pressing lightly.

8 Deep fry in hot oil over a medium heat until the sesame seed balls are lightly browned.

Shilen toufu

(Almond jelly)

3 oz/80 g agar-agar or 1 oz/25 g gelatine ● 1¼ pt/750 ml water ●
½ lb/225 g sugar ● 8 fl oz/225 ml milk ● 1 tsp almond essence
For the puréed fruit toppings: ¼ melon and 1 tbsp sugar ● 2 fresh
or tinned peaches and 1 tbsp sugar

Shilen toufu is served with a puréed fruit topping (usually melon or peach juice). This is made by liquidizing each type of fruit separately with sugar in a blender.

1 Soften the agar-agar in a bowl of water for at least 1 hour changing the water from time to time. If using gelatine, soften it in a little hot water before adding it to the pan.

2 Squeeze the agar-agar and place in a pan with 1¼ pt/750 ml water. Stir constantly over a moderate heat until completely dissolved.

3 Add the sugar and stir until the sugar is dissolved.

4 Add the milk and remove from the heat as soon as boiling point is reached.

5 Add the almond essence. Stir and strain immediately through a cloth.

6 Allow to cool slightly and pour into small glasses, filling them three-quarters full. Place in the refrigerator to set. Pour the puréed fruit topping over each jelly before serving.

Two-colour lake dessert

For the Chinese cream: 2 tbsp white sesame seeds • 5 tbsp plain flour • 7 fl oz/200 ml water • 5 tbsp sugar
For the coloured balls: 3 oz/80 g rice flour • 3 fl oz/90 ml water • ½ tsp red food colouring

This Chinese dessert is served hot. The coloured balls floating in the cream give it its name. The Chinese cream (steps 1-4) is used as a base in many other Chinese recipes.

1 Toast the sesame seeds, taking care not to burn them. Place in a blender and grind coarsely.

2 Sieve the plain flour and heat gently in a pan, stirring with a wooden spoon, until lightly golden.

3 Add the water gradually to the flour and stir over a low heat. Add the sugar, stirring constantly, and cook until the cream thickens.

4 Add the toasted sesame seeds and stir.

5 Place the rice flour in a bowl and add the specified amount of water gradually, stirring until a thick paste is achieved.

6 Divide the paste in two; add the food colouring (dissolved in a little water) to one half and mix well to produce a pale pink colour.

7 Using both pastes (white and pink) make balls about ½ in/1.5 cm in diameter. Boil in water until they rise to the surface; drain well on a clean cloth.

8 Pour the cream into a serving dish and float the coloured balls on the surface. Serve hot.

Tea breads

Panettone milanese

1 oz/25 g yeast ● 2 lb/900 g flour ● ½ oz/15 g salt ● 7 oz/200 g melted butter ● 5 egg yolks ● 2 whole eggs ● 9 oz/250 g sugar, dissolved in a few tbsp hot water ● warm milk ● 3½ oz/100 g chopped candied peel ● 5 oz/150 g raisins soaked in brandy ● oil and butter to grease tin

Some experts maintain that panettone originated in Como, not in Milan. However, in the 19th century, bakers in Lombardy used to give a panettone to their customers at Christmas, thus establishing a tradition.

1 Make a paste with the yeast, 3½ oz/100 g flour and sufficient lukewarm water to bind into a dough. Leave this mixture to rise in a soft cloth until doubled in size. Weigh the ball of dough and add the same weight of flour, mixing in sufficient lukewarm water to make a dough again. Leave to rise until doubled in size.

Repeat the operation once more. (These three operations are known as 'strengthening the yeast' and should be carried out the day before the panettone is needed as they take 9-10 hours in all.)

2 Place the remaining flour in a heap, make a well in the centre and add the yeast mixture from step 1, the salt, melted butter, egg yolks, whole eggs and dissolved sugar. Knead for 10 minutes, gradually adding tepid milk until a soft dough is obtained. Work in the chopped candied peel and the raisins until they are evenly distributed and leave in a warm place to rise for about 6 hours.

3 Line a spring-release tin with greaseproof paper and grease well. Place the dough in the tin and make two cuts in the top in the shape of a cross. Brush with butter and bake in a pre-heated oven at 350°F/180°C/mark 4 for 30 minutes. The panettone is cooked when a skewer comes out clean.

Viennese ring

(Kugelhopf)

2 fl oz/60 ml milk ● 9 oz/250 g flour ● 1 whole egg ● ½ oz/15 g fresh yeast ● ½-1 oz/15-25 g candied peel, finely chopped ● 2 oz/50 g raisins ● 1 tsp grated lemon rind ● 3½ oz/100 g butter ● 3 oz/80 g icing sugar ● 2-3 egg yolks ● almond or hazelnuts, roughly chopped ● 1 egg and 1 tsp icing sugar to brush over ring ● knob of butter to grease mould

The basic dough for this recipe (containing flour, sugar, eggs, milk and yeast) makes a plain ring cake; by adding extra ingredients a wide variety of rings can be created. The *Saxon ring cake* contains aniseed: the *cherry ring cake* is an American favourite. The *Hamburg ring cake* contains almonds, cinnamon, candied fruit and ginger. The *Bremen ring cake* is similar to a fruit cake, though still ring-shaped. The *Dutch steamed ring cake* is cooked in a cloth like a Christmas pudding. The *French Royal Trianon ring cake* is filled with chocolate cream and covered with chocolate icing.

1 In a basin over simmering water work together the milk, flour, whole egg, yeast and chopped candied peel. Mix in the raisins and grated lemon rind. Allow to rest over the hot water.

2 In a separate bowl mix the butter, icing sugar and egg yolks.

3 Combine the two mixtures.

4 Cover with a cloth and leave to rise over hot water. The dough should double in size.

5 Butter a kugelhopf mould (this has a central tube and high, fluted sides and can be used for savarins and other desserts). Press the chopped nuts to the sides of the tin. Place the dough in the tin and allow to stand for 30 minutes.

6 Bake in a preheated oven at 350°F/180°C/mark 4 for about 1 hour. Unmould while still hot and brush with the egg beaten with a little icing sugar. Before serving sprinkle with icing sugar.

Fruit ring cake

For the dough: 2 tbsp ground almonds ● 3½ fl oz/100 ml milk ●
5 oz/150 g flour ● 3½ oz/100 g sugar ● 1 egg yolk ● 2 oz/50 g
softened butter ● 1 whole egg ● few drops vanilla essence ● 1 tsp
ground cinnamon ● 1 tsp ground ginger ● 3½ oz/100 g raisins ●
2 oz/50 g chopped candied peel ● few glacé cherries ● butter to
grease mould
For the rum glaze: 1 oz/25 g icing sugar ● rum
To decorate: walnut halves, candied peel and glacé cherries

1 Mix the ground almonds with the milk. Continuing to stir, add the flour, sugar, egg yolk, softened butter, whole egg and vanilla essence.

2 When the ingredients are well mixed and the dough soft and pliable place it on a floured board, add the cinnamon and ginger and knead until the spices are evenly worked in.

3 Flatten the dough with the palms of the hands, sprinkle the raisins, candied peel and glacé cherries on top. Form the dough into a ball with the fruit inside.

4 Generously butter a straight-sided ring mould.

5 Shape the dough to fit the ring and press into the buttered mould. Bake in a preheated oven at 400°F/ 200°C/mark 6 for 30 minutes.

6 Remove from the oven and allow to cool. While the cake is cooling prepare the rum glaze (see page 192). Spoon the glaze over the cake; before the glaze hardens decorate with walnut halves, candied peel and glacé cherries.

Carrot ring cake

For the dough: 3½ oz/100 g carrots • 2½ oz/70 g sugar • 3 egg yolks • 1½ oz/40 g flour • 2 oz/50 g ground almonds • 1 tsp grated lemon rind • 1 tbsp lemon juice • 3 egg whites • 2 tbsp Cointreau to soak cake • butter to grease and flour to dust mould
For the kirsch-flavoured buttercream: 1 oz/25 g icing sugar • 2 oz/50 g butter • 1 egg yolk • 1 tbsp kirsch
For the Chantilly cream: 7 fl oz/200 ml double cream • 1 oz/25 g icing sugar

This recipe is a variation on one of the most famous types of carrot cake, made in the canton of Aargau in Switzerland. This cake is sometimes covered with chocolate icing. The Aargau carrot cake is covered with kirsch-flavoured icing and is decorated with chopped, toasted almonds, then sprinkled with icing sugar.

1 Butter and flour a ring mould.

2 Peel and grate the carrots.

3 Place the sugar, egg yolks and flour in a basin over hot water and whisk until the mixture thickens.

4 Remove from the heat and stir in the carrots, ground almonds, grated lemon rind and lemon juice.

5 Whip the egg whites until stiff.

6 Fold carefully into the carrot mixture.

7 Pour half the mixture into the mould. Prepare the kirsch-flavoured buttercream (see page 187) and spread over the surface, then cover with the remaining mixture.

8 Bake in a preheated oven at 350°F/180°C/mark 4 for 45 minutes. Unmould and brush the top with Cointreau. Decorate with Chantilly cream (see page 190).

Fruit cake

2 oz/50 g butter ● 3 oz/80 g icing sugar ● ½ oz/15 g clear honey ● 2 eggs ● 3½ oz/100 g flour ● 1 tsp baking powder ● 9 oz/250 g raisins ● ½ oz/15 g walnuts, coarsely chopped ● 2-3 tbsp rum ● pinch cinnamon ● pinch nutmeg ● pinch allspice ● 1 oz/30 g chopped candied peel ● few glacé cherries ● butter to grease tin

The fruit cake was an English invention and is justly famous all over the world. The basic recipe can be adapted to give a range of variations: chopped almonds and pistachios can be added, or hazelnuts, or Brazil nuts. Ginger cake is another variation of the same recipe which differs from the other versions in that it contains no nuts or fruit, but is flavoured with ginger.

120

1 Cream the butter until light and smooth.

2 Stir in half the sugar a little at a time.

3 Stir in remaining sugar then add the honey.

4 Add the beaten eggs and mix well using a balloon whisk or electric beater.

5 Sift the flour with the baking powder and add to the mixture. Allow to rest.

6 Soak the raisins and walnuts for about 30 minutes in a mixture of the rum, brandy, cinnamon, nutmeg and allspice. Stir these ingredients together with the candied peel and glacé cherries into the mixture from step 5.

7 Line a rectangular cake tin with greaseproof paper buttered on both sides. Pour the mixture into the tin and smooth the surface with a spatula.

8 Bake in a preheated oven at 350°F/180°C/mark 4 for 1 hour or until cooked. The cake is cooked when a skewer inserted into the middle comes out clean.

Orange cake

5 oz/150 g icing sugar ● 5 oz/150 g butter ● 2 eggs ● 1 tsp grated orange rind ● few drops vanilla essence ● 5 oz/150 g flour ● 1 tsp baking powder ● 1 orange ● butter to grease and flour to dust tin

Unlike the preceding fruit cake this recipe uses fresh fruit rather than dried or candied fruit. The mixture rises more and is softer and less dense. The method and ingredients can be used to make many other delicious cakes with a variety of fresh fruit.

1 Butter a rectangular cake tin and dust with flour, shaking off the excess.

2 Sieve the icing sugar.

3 Cream the butter until light and smooth.

4 Add the sieved sugar gradually and mix well.

5 Lightly beat the eggs and stir into the mixture.

6 Add the grated orange rind and vanilla essence.

7 Add the flour and baking powder.

8 Peel the orange, divide into segments and remove pips. Pour one-third of the mixture into the cake tin and place half the orange segments on top; pour in another third of the mixture and cover with the remaining orange. Pour in the rest of the mixture. Leave to stand for about 30 minutes then bake in a preheated oven at 325°-350°F/170°-180°C/mark 3-4 for 60-70 minutes.

Brioches

For the dough: ½ oz/15 g fresh yeast ● 2 fl oz/60 ml milk or orange flower water ● 10½ oz/300 g flour ● 7 oz/200 g butter ● 1¼ oz/35 g sugar ● 1 tsp salt ● 3 eggs ● 1 beaten egg to brush brioches ● oil to grease moulds

The classic brioche is baked in a round fluted tin to produce the kind of brioche shown in the photograph. Brioches can be made in many different shapes and, although the dough is the same, they are named according to their shape. You can make coronets, small and large plaits, and so on.

1 Add the yeast to the milk or orange flower water with one-sixth of the flour. Allow to stand until doubled in volume.

2 Cream the butter.

3 Mix the remaining flour with the sugar and salt. Add the eggs and work into a paste.

4 When the paste is smooth add the yeast mixture from step 1.

5 Work in the creamed butter. Cover and leave in a warm place until doubled in volume (this will take about 10 hours).

6 Divide the dough into small balls. Brush the brioche tins with oil, fill each mould half full with the dough, shaping it so that there is a smaller ball on top.

7 Alternatively, pinch off a quarter of each dough ball, then make a dip in the centre with the fingers and place a tiny ball of dough (from the remaining quarter) in the dip.

8 Place the tins on a baking tray. Brush the brioches with beaten egg. Bake in a preheated oven at 450°F/230°C/mark 8 for 10-20 minutes until golden. Remove from the oven, unmould and allow to cool.

Brioche croissants

½ oz/15 g fresh yeast • 2 fl oz/60 ml milk or orange flower water • 10½ oz/300 g flour • 1 oz/25 g sugar • 1 tsp salt • 1 whole egg • 1 egg yolk • 3½-5 fl oz/100 ml milk • 2 oz/50 g butter • 3½-5 oz/100-150 g softened butter • 1 egg, beaten with 1 tsp icing sugar to brush brioches • butter to grease and flour to dust tray

Croissants, like brioches, are of French origin but are known all over the world. The main difference between croissants and brioches is the crescent shape of the croissants. They can also be filled with cream or jam, as are the German *Kipfel*.

This recipe is entitled 'brioche croissants'; in France it would simply be 'croissants' since croissants are generally made with a brioche dough and are smooth, soft and light. Croissants can also be made with flaky pastry. For flaky pastry recipe *see page 193.*

1 Mix the yeast with the milk or orange flower water and a few spoonfuls of flour.

2 Make a well in the centre of the remaining flour and mix in the sugar, salt, whole egg and yolk, milk and 2 oz/50 g butter.

3 Add the yeast mixture from step 1 and mix thoroughly.

4 Cover and leave to rise in a warm place until doubled in volume.

5 Roll out the dough with a rolling pin.

6 Spread the softened butter over a third of the dough with a spatula.

7 Fold the dough in three and roll out again. Place in the refrigerator for 15 minutes. Fold in three again and roll out with the rolling pin. Leave to rest in the refrigerator for another 15 minutes.

8 Roll out the dough to about ¾ in/2 cm thick and cut into triangles. Starting from the base roll up each triangle and curve into a crescent shape. Place on a buttered, floured baking tray and brush with egg beaten with a little icing sugar. Bake in a preheated oven at 450°F/230°C/mark 8 for 20 minutes.

127

Raisin bread

2¼ lb/1 kg flour ● 1 tsp salt ● 2 oz/50 g fresh yeast ● 5 fl oz/ 150 ml tepid milk ● 7 oz/200 g softened butter ● 5 oz/150 g raisins, soaked in a small glass of Marsala ● 9 oz/250 g sugar ● 2 oz/50 g pine-nuts ● 1 oz/25 g pistachios, coarsely chopped ● 1 oz/25 g chopped candied peel ● butter to grease baking tray

Raisin bread is a traditional Italian sweet which is made for Christmas, New Year and Epiphany in Liguria. Its fame has spread far beyond Italian shores and it is more commonly known as 'Genoese sweet bread'; another well-known variety is made with raisins, but without nuts.

1 Sift the flour and salt into a mound and make a well in the centre. Crumble the yeast into the well with a little tepid milk, work into a paste then add the other ingredients.

2 Knead well, adding a little more tepid milk if necesary. Knead for 15-20 minutes.

3 Wrap in a floured cloth and leave to rise in a warm place for about 12 hours until doubled in volume.

4 Place the dough in a round loaf shape on a buttered baking tray. Make three triangular cuts on top (this is the traditional way of marking this bread, like the two crosses on the panettone). Bake in a preheated oven at 350°F/ 180°C/mark 4 for about 1 hour.

Biscuits

Sponge fingers

5 oz/150 g sugar • 6 egg yolks • 5 oz/150 g flour • 1 tsp salt • 6 egg whites • icing sugar and caster sugar to sprinkle on biscuits • butter to grease and flour to dust baking tray

1 Beat the sugar and egg yolks until creamy. Continuing to beat, gradually add the flour and salt.

2 Whisk the egg whites until they form stiff peaks. Fold carefully into the mixture, stirring from bottom to top until well mixed.

3 Using a piping bag with a wide plain nozzle pipe the dough into strips 4 in/10 cm long on a well-buttered and floured baking tray.

4 Mix the two kinds of sugar and sprinkle over the fingers.

5 Bake in a preheated oven at 325°F/170°C/mark 3 for 15-20 minutes.

Scones

1¼ lb/600 g flour • 1 tsp baking powder • ½ tsp salt • 1 tbsp grated orange (or lemon) rind • 3 oz/80 g softened butter • 2¾ oz/75 g sugar • 2 eggs • 10-12 fl oz/300-350 ml single cream or milk • butter to grease baking tray

The recipe given here is for scones enriched with eggs and cream, though the basic recipe uses only flour, baking powder, butter, milk and a pinch of salt. Scones are eaten warm or cold, usually spread with butter and jam, or cheese, either at breakfast or at tea-time. Variations on the basic recipe include cheese scones, and scones with dried fruit or candied peel.

1 Sift the flour together with the baking powder and salt into a basin; add the grated orange rind.

2 Work in the softened butter.

3 Add the sugar and mix until well blended.

4 Add one egg and the cream or milk and knead lightly to make a soft dough.

5 Place the dough in a bowl and allow to rest for about 1 hour.

6 Roll out the dough to a thickness of about ¾ in/2 cm. Cut out the scones with a round pastry cutter. Transfer to a buttered baking tray. Brush the surface of the scones with the remaining beaten egg.

7 Bake in a preheated oven at 400°F/200°C/mark 6 for 10-12 minutes.

Macaroons

10½ oz/300 g whole almonds or ready-ground ● 1¼ oz/35 g bitter almonds ● 11 oz/325 g sugar ● few drops vanilla essence ● 4 egg whites ● butter to grease and flour to dust baking tray

Some people, misled by the fact that the industrial production of macaroons began in Lombardy in Italy, regard the macaroon as a Lombard sweetmeat. In fact, the macaroon was originally made in Sicily although it is now eaten world-wide. Descended from the Sicilian macaroon and equally well-known, at least in Europe, is the Coburg macaroon (from Upper Bavaria), which contains whole eggs, honey, cocoa and spices, hazelnut flour and candied peel. In France macaroons are decorated with royal icing.

1 Place the almonds in boiling water for a few minutes until the skins can be removed without difficulty. Peel the almonds and place in a warm oven (it should not be alight) to dry without toasting. Grind the almonds fairly finely.

2 Add the sugar and the vanilla essence to the almonds.

3 Mix the egg whites one by one into the ingredients to make a soft, well-blended paste.

4 Using a piping bag with a round plain nozzle pipe drops of mixture 2 in/5 cm in diameter on a buttered and floured baking tray.

5 Bake in a preheated oven at 300°F/150°C/mark 2 for 20-30 minutes.

Cheese straws

6 oz/175 g flour • pinch nutmeg • pinch white pepper • pinch salt • 5 oz/150 g softened butter • 2 oz/50 g Cheddar cheese • 1 egg • 2 fl oz/60 ml milk • butter to grease and flour to dust baking tray

Cheese straws can be made with Cheddar, Cheshire or any leftover hard cheese. In Switzerland there is a similar recipe for biscuits made with Sbrinz cheese. Cheese straws are generally eaten with an aperitif, or as a snack.

1 Sift together the flour, nutmeg, pepper and salt.

2 Cream the butter with a wooden spoon until pale and smooth.

3 Grate the cheese and mix in with the butter.

4 Beat the egg and add to the cheese and butter mixture.

5 Stir in the milk gradually and mix well.

6 Add the dry ingredients from step 1.

7 Spoon the mixture into a piping bag with a fluted or star-shaped nozzle. Pipe strips 3-4 in/8-10 cm long on to a buttered and floured baking tray.

8 Bake in a preheated oven at 400°F/200°C/mark 6 for 10-15 minutes. Cool the cheese straws on a wire rack.

135

Fancy biscuits
Chocolate men

For the fancy biscuits: 4½ oz/140 g butter ● 4½ oz/140 g sugar ● 4 egg yolks ● 1 tsp or 3 tablets cream of tartar ● 9 oz/250 g flour ● ½ tsp salt ● caster sugar to coat biscuits ● butter to grease baking tray

1 Cream the butter until light and pale.

2 Stir in the sugar and mix well.

3 Add the egg yolks one at a time.

4 Mix thoroughly until the ingredients are blended.

5 If using tablets of cream of tartar crumble them with a rolling pin or pestle.

6 Sift the cream of tartar together with the flour and salt.

7 Add the dry ingredients to the mixture from step 4.

8 Mix lightly with a spatula.

9 As the mixture becomes harder to work, stir with a wooden spoon until it is well blended. It should still be quite crumbly.

10 Place the dough in a large bowl, cover with cling film and allow to stand for a couple of hours.

11 Flour the working surface.

12 To avoid the pastry breaking up because it is so crumbly, work the pastry in three separate pieces.

13 Make a ball or block of each of the three pieces of pastry and sprinkle generously with flour.

14 Roll out with the rolling pin into three sheets.

15 If the sheets of pastry stick to the board, use a broad spatula or dough scraper to free them.

16 Roll the pastry out about ¼ in/5 mm thick.

17 Cut the biscuits into shapes with decorative cutters.

18 Dip both sides of the biscuits in sugar and place on a buttered baking tray. Bake in a preheated oven at 350°F/180°C/mark 4 for 15 minutes.

15

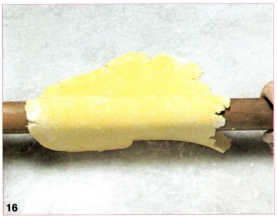

16

17

18

For the chocolate men: 9 oz/250 g flour ● pinch salt ● 1 tsp bicarbonate of soda ● 1 tsp ginger ● 2 oz/50 g sugar ● 3½ oz/ 100 g chocolate ● 2 fl oz/60 ml water ● 1¾ fl oz/50 ml milk ● 3 oz/ 80 g butter ● royal icing (see page 192) ● butter to grease baking tray

19

20

21

19 Sift together the flour, salt, bicarbonate of soda, ginger and sugar.

20 Melt the chocolate with the water in a pan over a low heat. Add the melted chocolate, milk and softened butter to the dry ingredients from step 19. Work together to form a smooth dough, then cover and leave to stand for a couple of hours.

21 Roll out the dough to a thickness of ¼ in/5 mm. Cut out the biscuits using cutters in the shape of people (or other shapes such as numbers or letters). Place the biscuits on a buttered baking tray and bake in a preheated oven at 350°F/ 180°C/mark 4 for 12-15 minutes. Remove from the oven and put on a wire rack to cool. Decorate with royal icing, if desired.

Jam drops

5 oz/150 g butter ● 5 oz/150 g sugar ● 2 eggs ● 1 tsp grated lemon rind ● 2 tbsp Marsala ● 7 oz/200 g flour ● 2-3 oz/50-80 g apricot jam ● butter to grease baking tray

1 Cream the butter in a basin and stir in the sugar gradually. Add the eggs, lemon rind and Marsala and mix well. Shake the flour in gradually through a sieve, stirring until well blended. (If the dough is too firm add a few more teaspoons of Marsala.)

2 Allow to stand for an hour or two.

3 Use your hands to shape the dough into small balls about the size of walnuts. Place the dough balls on a buttered baking tray and flatten each one with the base of a glass to make

'drops' 1¼ in/3 cm in diameter. Make a well in the centre of each one with your finger and fill with 1 tsp jam.

4 Bake in a preheated oven at 350°F/180°C/mark 4 for 15 minutes.

Peanut biscuits

5 oz/150 g butter ● 4 oz/125 g sugar (half white and half brown) ● 2¼ oz/60 g finely ground peanuts ● 1 egg ● 1 tsp grated orange rind ● 5½ oz/160 g flour ● pinch baking powder ● 1 egg yolk to glaze ● butter to grease baking tray

1 Cream the butter and the sugar.

2 Stir in the ground peanuts.

3 Add the egg and grated orange rind and mix until smooth.

4 Stir in the flour and baking powder gradually, preferably letting it fall through a sieve.

5 Allow to rest for 1 hour.

6 Roll out ¼ in/5 mm thick. Using a crinkle-edged cutter about 1½-2 in / 4-5 cm in diameter cut out the biscuits.

7 Place on a buttered baking tray.

8 Using a fork, make criss-cross stripes on the surface, as shown in the photograph.

9 Brush with egg yolk and bake in a preheated oven at 350°F/180°C/mark 4 for 15 minutes.

Almond paste wheels and rings

3½ oz/100 g butter • 9 oz/250 g sugar • 10½ oz/300 g ground almonds • 1 whole egg • 4 egg whites • 1 tsp grated lemon or orange rind • few tbsp potato flour or cornflour • butter to grease baking tray • 3½ oz/100 g chopped candied fruit

Where almond paste is concerned, the pâtisserie of Sicily leads the way. This recipe is only one of the many uses for this paste; almond paste originated in Sicily, with its age-old tradition of pâtisserie, and is now known all over the world. (See also page 187.)

1 Cream together the butter and sugar.

2 Add the ground almonds and mix well.

3 Beat in the whole egg, then the egg whites one by one.

4 Add the grated lemon or orange rind.

5 If the dough is too soft add a few tbsp potato flour until the pastry is quite firm.

6 Place the dough in a piping bag with a star-shaped nozzle ½ in/1 cm wide.

7 Butter a baking tray. Pipe the dough on to the tray. For the wheel-shaped biscuits, squeeze out some of the dough in a single action, as shown in the photograph. For the rings, pipe a circle of dough so that the ends overlap.

8 Press one or two pieces of candied fruit on to each biscuit and leave to stand overnight. Bake in a preheated oven at 350°F/180°C/mark 4 for 15 minutes, until lightly golden.

Chocolate chip biscuits
Oatmeal biscuits

For the chocolate chip biscuits: 5 oz/150 g sugar • 2¾ oz/75 g butter • few drops vanilla essence • 6 oz/175 g flour • ½ tsp salt • 1 tsp baking powder • 1 egg, beaten • 3½ oz/100 g chocolate chips • 2 oz/50 g chopped walnuts • butter to grease and flour to dust baking tray

Some biscuits, made with flour, sugar and eggs are so simple even a child could make them. To the basic recipe for these biscuits a great range of ingredients can be added; even the type of flour used can be varied: instead of ordinary flour you can use oatmeal, maize flour, nut flours such as almond, walnut or peanut, ground aduki beans and so on.

For the oatmeal biscuits: 2 oz/50 g caster sugar ● 3½ oz/100 g brown sugar ● 3½ oz/100 g butter or margarine ● few drops vanilla essence ● 3½ oz/100 g flour ● ½ tsp salt ● ½ tsp bicarbonate of soda ● 1 egg, beaten ● 2¾ oz/75 g oatmeal, toasted and ground to flour ● 2 oz/50 g chopped walnuts ● butter to grease and flour to dust baking tray

1 For the chocolate chip biscuits: mix the sugar, butter and vanilla essence together.

2 Stir in the flour, salt and baking powder.

3 Add the beaten egg and stir until smooth.

4 Add the chopped walnuts and chocolate chips and mix well.

5 Butter a baking tray and sprinkle with flour. Spoon out small heaps of dough at regular intervals and bake in a preheated oven at 350°F/180°C/mark 4 for 10-12 minutes.

6 For the oatmeal biscuits: mix the ingredients following instructions for steps 1, 2 and 3, adding the bicarbonate of soda instead of the baking powder in step 2. Stir in the oatmeal.

7 Add the chopped walnuts and mix well. Follow step 5.

Almond drops

4½ oz/140 g margarine or butter, softened ● 4 oz/125 g sugar ● 7 oz/200 g flour ● few drops vanilla essence ● ½ tsp salt ● 1 egg ● 1 egg yolk, mixed with 1 tbsp water ● 25-30 almonds, halved ● butter to grease baking tray

Almonds have many uses in pâtisserie. They are frequently used in all kinds of desserts, creams and biscuits. They can be toasted and salted and eaten with cocktails; they can be pralined or caramelized or used in confectionery. They are an essential ingredient in nougat; also in marzipan, almond paste and almond milk.

146

1 Cream the margarine in a bowl.

2 Beat in the sugar a little at a time.

3 Continuing to stir, add the flour, vanilla essence and salt.

4 Add the egg and work to a paste. Place in the refrigerator to rest for 2 hours.

5 With your hands shape the dough into balls about 1¼ in/3 cm in diameter and place on a buttered baking tray.

6 Flatten each ball with the base of a glass to make a 'drop'.

7 Brush with egg yolk diluted with 1 tbsp water.

8 Place an almond half on each biscuit. Bake in a preheated oven at 350°F/180°C/mark 4 for 10 minutes.

Cats' tongues

4½ oz/140 g butter • 6 oz/175 g flour • 4½ oz/140 g icing sugar
• few drops vanilla essence • 2 egg whites • butter to grease and
flour to dust baking tray

1 Cream the butter in a bowl.

2 Stirring constantly, add the flour and sugar (preferably through a sieve) and the vanilla essence.

3 Whisk the egg whites and fold carefully into the mixture, stirring from bottom to top. (If the dough is not soft enough add another beaten egg white.)

4 Spoon the dough into a piping bag with a wide plain nozzle.

5 On a heavy buttered and floured baking tray (the bottom of the biscuits will burn if it is not heavy) pipe the dough into 3½-4 in/ 9-10 cm lengths. Leave plenty of space between the biscuits to prevent them spreading during cooking and joining together.

6 Bake in a preheated oven at 400°F/200°C/mark 6 for 5 minutes. The biscuits are ready when the edges begin to turn golden. Place on a wire rack to cool.

148

Mother-in-law's tongues with almonds

9 oz/250 g whole almonds or flaked almonds • 3½ fl oz/100 ml single cream • 2 egg yolks • 9 oz/250 g icing sugar • 2¾ oz/75 g flour • 1 tsp baking powder • 2 egg whites • butter to grease and flour to dust baking tray

1 Soak the almonds in boiling water for 5-10 minutes until their skins peel off easily. Slice them lengthwise as finely as possible.

2 Mix the cream and egg yolks together in a bowl.

3 Sift the dry ingredients into the mixture, in the following order, stirring continuously: sugar, flour and baking powder.

4 Whisk the egg whites and fold carefully into the mixture, stirring from bottom to top. If the dough is too soft add a little more flour. Allow to stand for several hours.

5 Butter a heavy baking tray and dust with flour (if it is not heavy enough the base of the biscuits will burn).

6 Spoon the dough into a piping bag with a wide plain nozzle. Pipe on to the baking tray in strips 2 in/5 cm long, spacing them well in order to prevent them sticking together during cooking.

7 Cover each strip with almond flakes.

8 Bake in a preheated oven at 400°F/200°C/mark 6 for 5 minutes. Remove from the tray at once and shape the biscuits on a rolling pin or metal tube for a few seconds before placing them on a wire rack to cool.

149

Tea biscuits

For the plain biscuits: 7 oz/200 g butter • 2¾ oz/75 g icing sugar •
1 egg white • 9 oz/250 g flour • 1 tsp baking powder • butter to
grease baking tray

1 Take the butter out of the
refrigerator a couple of
hours in advance so that it
will be soft and easy to
work. Cream the butter and
sugar; whisk the egg white
and fold in carefully, stirring
from bottom to top.

2 Add the flour and the
baking powder and mix
until the dough is smooth
and stiff.

3 Leave to stand for 1 hour
in a container covered with
cling film.

4 Knead the dough lightly
on a floured surface.

5 Roll the dough into
cylinders about 1½ in/4 cm
in diameter.

6 Cut into ½ in/1 cm slices

with a sharp knife. Place on
a buttered baking tray and
bake in a preheated oven at
325°F/170°C/mark 3 for a
maximum of 10 minutes
(keep a careful watch as
they will begin to brown
very quickly).

For the two-coloured squares: 9 oz/250 g flour • 1 tsp baking powder • 4½ oz/140 g softened butter • 4½ oz/140 g icing sugar • 4 egg yolks • few drops vanilla essence • 1 oz/25 g cocoa powder • 1 egg yolk mixed with 1 tbsp water to glaze biscuits • sugar to sprinkle over the biscuits

7 Make a dough with all the ingredients except the cocoa powder and the egg yolk for glazing. If the dough is too soft add more flour. Divide off one-third of the dough. Add the cocoa powder to two thirds of the dough.

8 Roll the light-coloured dough into a cylinder 8 in/20 cm long. Roll half the dark dough into a cylinder the same length. Flatten both cylinders, light and dark, as illustrated.

9 Cut the flattened pieces in half lengthwise.

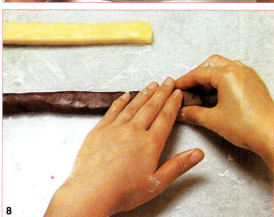

10 With the remaining dark dough roll out a rectangle large enough to enclose all the cylinders once. Brush the dough with the diluted egg yolk. Place one of the cylinders three-quarters of the way down the sheet of dough and brush with egg yolk. Place a second cylinder of dough (of a different colour) next to the first and brush with egg yolk.

11 Place the other two cylinders on top, alternating the colours, and brush with egg.

12 Roll the cylinders in the dough and cut away any excess.

13 Cut the rolls into slices ½ in/1 cm thick and sprinkle with sugar. Place on a buttered baking tray. Bake in a preheated oven at 375°F/190°C/mark 5 for 10 minutes. You can devise other variations on the two-coloured biscuits.

For the coconut fingers: 4½ oz/140 g finely ground coconut
● 5¾ oz/170 g softened butter ● 5¾ oz/170 g sugar ●
1 egg ● 10 oz/275 g flour ● 1 tsp baking powder ● 1 egg
yolk mixed with 1 tbsp water ● grated coconut to decorate
● cinnamon mixed with sugar to sprinkle over biscuits

14 Spread the coconut on a baking tray and toast in a preheated oven at 275°F/140°C/mark 1 until the coconut begins to colour (be careful not to allow it to brown excessively). Allow to cool.

15 Cream the butter, then beat in the sugar followed by the egg.

16 Sift the flour and the baking powder and gradually stir into the egg mixture. Add the ground coconut from step 14 and mix well.

17 Place a piece of cling film on a baking tray measuring about 6 × 8 in/15 × 20 cm. Spread the dough on the cling film in a rectangle about ½ in/1 cm thick.

18 Smooth the top carefully and trim the corners and edges. Brush with the diluted egg yolk and sprinkle over the grated coconut.

19 Sprinkle the surface with cinnamon sugar. Cover with a sheet of cling film and place in the freezer to harden for at least 2 hours.

20 Remove the two sheets of cling film. Place the dough on a board, and cut into strips ½ in/1 cm wide and 2 in/5 cm long. Place on a baking tray covered with baking parchment or grease with butter. Bake in a preheated oven at 325°F/170°C/mark 3 for 15-20 minutes. Cool on a wire rack.

Almond crackers

2 egg whites • 2 oz/50 g icing sugar • ½ oz/15 g potato flour or cornflour • 2 oz/50 g ground almonds

1 Whisk the egg whites. Sift the sugar and potato flour and beat into the egg whites using a metal whisk.

2 The mixture should be very stiff, forming peaks when lifted. Add the ground almonds.

3 Mix until smooth.

4 Place a sheet of baking parchment on a baking tray. Using a rectangular biscuit cutter measuring 1-2 × 3-4 in/3-5 × 8-10 cm make biscuits shaped as illustrated ⅛ in/3 mm thick.

5 When the baking tray is filled, place in a preheated oven at 450°F/230°C/mark 8 for 5 minutes.

6 Remove the crackers from the baking tray at once with a spatula and place on a wire rack to cool.

Almond crescents

5 oz/150 g almonds ● 5 oz/150 g butter ● 2 oz/50 g icing sugar ●
2 fl oz/60 ml brandy ● 7 oz/200 g flour

There are thousands of different recipes for almond
biscuits the world over. The ingredients given here can
be made into any shape you fancy.

1 Chop the almonds coarsely. Toast them on a baking tray in a low oven.

2 Cream together the butter and the sugar.

3 Add the brandy.

4 Add the flour and the chopped, toasted almonds; stir until the ingredients are well blended.

5 Allow to rest in a container for 30 minutes.

6 Knead the dough lightly, form into a rectangle and divide into sections. Roll and flatten each section and cut into small, equal pieces.

7 Roll the pieces one by one in the palm of your hand.

8 Place on a buttered baking tray and shape into crescents. Bake in a preheated oven at 325°F/170°C/mark 3 for 15 minutes.

Madeleines

2½ oz/70 g butter • 2¼ oz/60 g icing sugar • 2 egg yolks •
2 tbsp brandy • 2 egg whites • 1½ oz/40 g flour • pinch salt •
¾ oz/20 g potato flour or cornflour • few drops vanilla essence •
melted butter to grease moulds

This is a classic French recipe from Alsace. The traditional moulds are shell-shaped. Smaller moulds are often used, the resulting biscuits being called *madeleinettes*. When cooled, madeleines or madeleinettes can be iced with lemon icing (see page 192).

1 Brush the madeleine moulds with a little melted butter.

2 Melt the 2½ oz/70 g butter over hot water.

3 Sift the sugar to eliminate lumps.

4 In a basin over simmering water mix together the sugar, egg yolks, and brandy and stir until thick. Remove from the heat and transfer the mixture to another bowl to cool.

5 Beat the egg whites and blend in the flour and salt. Fold in mixture from step 4.

6 Add the potato flour and vanilla essence and mix well.

7 Add the melted butter from step 2 and mix well.

8 Pour the dough into the buttered moulds. Bake in a preheated oven at 400°F/200°C/mark 6 for about 10 minutes. Remove from the moulds at once and cool on a wire rack.

Vanilla crescents

5 oz/150 g butter • 3½ oz/100 g flour • 3½ oz/100 g potato flour or cornflour • 3½ oz/100 g ground almonds • 2¼ oz/60 g sugar • greaseproof paper for baking tray • vanilla-flavoured icing sugar

1 Soften the butter at room temperature and cream with a balloon whisk until pale and light.

2 Sieve the flour and potato flour together in a separate bowl and mix with the ground almonds and

sugar. Add to the creamed butter and mix thoroughly until a smooth dough is obtained.

3 Shape the dough into rolls about ½ in/1 cm thick then cut into 2-in/5-cm segments.

4 Cover a baking tray with greaseproof paper. Place the segments of dough on the tray and shape them into crescents.

5 Bake in a preheated oven at 400°F/200°C/mark 6 for 15 minutes.

6 Remove from the oven and roll the biscuits in vanilla-flavoured icing sugar.

Creams, mousses, soufflés, ice-cream

Cream caramel

6 oz/125 g sugar • 7 egg yolks • 3 egg whites • few drops vanilla essence • 18 fl oz/500 ml milk

1 To make the caramel, heat 2 oz/50 g sugar in a pan with a few tsp water, stirring until the syrup turns light brown. Remove from the heat and use immediately.

2 Pour equal quantities of caramel into small moulds.

3 Beat the egg yolks and remaining sugar together in a large bowl until thick and creamy.

4 Whisk the egg whites until very stiff and fold into the egg and sugar mixture.

5 Add the vanilla essence to the milk and bring to the boil. Allow to cool a little, then pour into the egg mixture and mix well.

6 Place the moulds in a baking tin and fill with water to come half-way up the sides of the moulds.

7 Divide the custard between the moulds, pouring it through a sieve first to eliminate any lumps.

8 Place the tin in a preheated oven at 325°F/170°C/mark 3 for 20-30 minutes or until the custards are firm.

9 Stand them in a cool place for several hours or overnight.

10 Cream caramel can be served with tinned peaches or apricots or with whipped or single cream.

Wine jelly
Coffee jelly

¾ oz/20 g leaf or powdered gelatine ● 2 oz/50 g icing sugar ● 7 fl oz/
200 ml water ● 9 fl oz/250 ml red wine ● 2 oz/50 g clear honey
● pinch of cinnamon ● 2 cups strong black coffee
To decorate the coffee jelly: double cream

Just before serving turn out the wine jellies into individual dishes and pour over any remaining wine and honey mixture prepared in step 6. Before serving the coffee jelly decorate with double cream.

1 Prepare the gelatine in a little hot water.

2 Dissolve the sugar with the 7 fl oz/200 ml water in a pan over a low heat.

3 Remove from the heat, add the gelatine and stir.

4 When the ingredients are blended pour through a sieve.

5 Divide the mixture equally between two bowls. Boil the wine with the honey and a pinch of cinnamon and allow to reduce slightly.

Add the coffee to one bowl and three-quarters of the wine mixture to the other.

6 Mix well and divide equally between jelly moulds. Leave to set.

Vanilla bavarois

¾ oz/20 g gelatine • 18 fl oz/500 ml milk • 9 oz/250 g caster sugar
• 6 egg yolks • 1 tsp cornflour • 1 tbsp vanilla sugar • 18 fl oz/
500 ml double cream • almond or sunflower oil to brush mould

A bavarois is similar in consistency to a cream caramel. A ring mould should be used to ensure that the consistency of the dessert is the same throughout. This classic vanilla bavarois may be used as a basic recipe; alternative flavours may be achieved by adding melted chocolate, instant coffee dissolved in a little water, liqueurs or fortified wines such as Marsala, or fruit (for example strawberries, banana, candied fruit, melon). Fruit-flavoured bavarois can be accompanied by mixed, sliced fruit.

1 Sprinkle the gelatine into a little hot water in a cup to dissolve it.

2 Reserve a small glass of milk; put the rest of the milk and sugar in a saucepan over a low heat.

3 With a balloon whisk, beat the egg yolks, cornflour and vanilla sugar. Add the reserved cold milk. When the milk in the saucepan comes to the boil add it to the egg mixture.

4 Return the mixture to the heat; when it is almost at boiling point, remove and stir in the gelatine. Do not allow to boil.

5 Leave to cool, stirring occasionally.

6 Whip the cream and fold gently into the mixture. Turn into a mould which has been brushed with almond or sunflower oil. Refrigerate for at least 5 hours before serving.

Meringues

2 oz/50 g caster sugar for each egg white

The word *meringue* generally refers to a sweet made with stiffly whisked egg whites and sugar, cooked in a slow oven until firm.

This basic recipe can be used to make various different shapes – ovals, cones and so on – in a variety of colours, depending on the flavouring added, for example chocolate, coffee, nuts.

Alternatively, the meringue can be shaped into a nest, serving as a flan base, and can be filled with whipped cream, ice-cream, custard or fruit.

Meringue arranged in layers with sponge cake, butter-cream, fruit and whipped cream makes an elegant and delicious party dessert.

1 Whisk the egg whites as stiffly as possible using a balloon whisk or electric beater. A fork, which is often used for beating eggs for pancakes and omelettes, is not suitable in this case.

2 Sieve the sugar and fold in carefully so that the whites do not collapse.

3 Place the mixture in small heaps on a greased baking sheet, using either a spoon or a piping bag with a large plain nozzle.

4 Bake immediately in a preheated oven at 225°F/ 110° C/ mark ¼ until firm and dry.

167

Carrot halwa

(Indian carrot jelly)

1¼ lb/600 g carrots ● 1¼ pt/750 ml milk ● ½ tsp saffron ● 2 oz/50 g butter ● 2 oz/50 g icing sugar ● 2 tbsp clear honey ● ½ tsp ground cinnamon ● ½ oz/15 g powdered gelatine
To decorate (optional): 2 tbsp almonds, coarsely chopped ● 1 banana, thinly sliced

1 Peel, wash and grate the carrots.

2 Boil the carrots in the milk for 1¼ hours until thick and creamy.

3 Add the saffron, butter, sugar, honey and cinnamon and stir well.

4 Cook for a further 10 minutes.

5 Dissolve the gelatine in 1-2 tbsp hot water; add to the carrot mixture.

6 Pour the mixture into moulds and allow to cool and set.

7 Before serving, decorate with chopped almonds and slices of banana, if desired.

Yogurt jelly

6 tsp icing sugar • 5 fl oz/150 ml yogurt • 2 tbsp Maraschino or similar sweet liqueur • 3½ fl oz/100 ml double cream • ½ oz/15 g gelatine • 2½ fl oz/75 ml water
To decorate: 1 lime • fresh mint leaves

1 Mix the sugar and the yogurt. Add the Maraschino and stir.

2 Whip the cream until stiff, then fold the cream carefully into the yogurt.

3 Dissolve the gelatine in the hot water and add gradually to the yogurt mixture.

4 Pour the jelly into moulds.

5 Place in the refrigerator.

6 Turn out the jellies into individual glass dishes.

7 Decorate with slices of lime and fresh mint leaves.

Cointreau jellies
with orange sauce

½ oz/15 g leaf or powdered gelatine • 2 fl oz/60 ml hot water •
2 oz/50 g sugar • 2 egg yolks • ½ pt/300 ml milk • 2-3 tbsp
Cointreau • 2 egg whites
For the orange sauce: 2 oz/50 g sugar • juice of 5 oranges

To make the orange sauce, dissolve the sugar in the orange juice over a low heat. Bring to the boil, then remove from the heat. Allow to cool. To serve, turn out the individual moulds on to a serving dish and pour round the orange sauce.

1 Put the gelatine and the hot water in a bowl to soften the gelatine.

2 Beat together the sugar and egg yolks until creamy. Add the milk and mix.

3 Add the gelatine and the liqueur.

4 Keep the mixture warm over a bowl of hot water until needed.

5 Beat the egg whites until stiff.

6 Fold carefully into the cream, stirring carefully from bottom to top.

7 Pour into moulds and allow to set.

8 Prepare the orange sauce (see method opposite).

Mint cream

½ oz/15 g leaf or powdered gelatine ● 3 egg yolks ● 3½ oz/100 g icing sugar ● 7 fl oz/200 ml tepid milk ● 3 tbsp mint syrup (ready-made or see step 4, below) ● 5 fl oz/150 ml double cream
To decorate: 6 green Maraschino cherries

1 Soak the gelatine in a small glass of hot water.

2 Beat the egg yolks and sugar until creamy.

3 Add the tepid milk and mix.

4 Add the mint syrup (made by boiling a little water with sugar and fresh mint leaves until syrupy, then straining). Mix.

5 Add the gelatine and keep the mixture warm over

a pan of hot water until step 6 is completed.

6 Whip the cream until stiff.

7 Fold the cream into the mint mixture, stirring carefully.

8 Pour into a large fluted mould. Allow to cool and set.

9 Before serving turn out and decorate with green Maraschino cherries.

Trifle with meringue topping

1 pt/600 ml confectioner's custard (see page 15, steps 1-4) • 10½ oz/300 g sponge (see page 194) or sponge fingers (see page 131) • few drops of cochineal (red food colouring) mixed with 2 fl oz/60 ml water or liqueur of your choice • 5 oz/150 g candied fruit, diced or chopped mixed peel • 2 fl oz/60 ml rum to soak sponge • 5 egg whites • 5 oz/150 g icing sugar • glacé cherries • 1 oz/25 g almonds, roughly chopped (optional)

This recipe, which uses a meringue topping, is a variation on the classic trifle covered with sweetened whipped cream.

1 Place 5 tbsp of the confectioner's custard in a large, ovenproof glass dish and place on top half the sponge, cut into large squares and sprinkle with the cochineal or liqueur. Cover with another layer of custard and four-fifths of the candied fruit.

2 Cover with a second layer of sponge, sprinkled with rum, and the remaining custard.

3 Prepare the meringue topping by whipping the egg whites and carefully folding in the icing sugar. Cover the sponge with the meringue and decorate with the remaining candied fruit, glacé cherries and almonds.

4 Place in a moderate oven (350°F/180°C/mark 4) for 3-5 minutes to brown the meringue.

5 Serve well chilled.

173

Blancmange

5 oz/150 g icing sugar • 3 oz/80 g cornflour • ½ pt/300 ml hot milk • 2 tbsp white Curaçao • 7 fl oz/200 ml single cream • 3½ fl oz/ 100 ml almond milk (see below)

Blancmange is a classic French dessert. The basic ingredients are not always identical: sometimes the cream is left out, sometimes no liqueur is used. One essential ingredient, however, is the almond milk, made by pounding or liquidizing 4 oz/125 g almonds with 3½ fl oz/100 ml water and squeezing the liquid through a cloth. The blancmange mixture is poured into small moulds and left in the refrigerator to set until needed.

1 Sieve the sugar and cornflour together into a bowl.

2 Dissolve the sugar and cornflour in a ladleful of milk.

3 Add the remaining milk.

4 Stir the mixture in a pan over a low heat until it thickens.

5 Add the Curaçao, then stir in the cream.

6 Stir in the almond milk. Pour the mixture into

moulds. Allow to cool and set in the refrigerator for several hours.

Cream cheese mousse

7 oz/200 g cream cheese • ½ oz/15 g powdered or leaf gelatine • 1 pt 3½ fl oz/700 ml hot milk • 3½ fl oz/100 ml whipped cream • 1 tsp grated lemon rind • juice of ½ a lemon • 1 tbsp white Curaçao • 3 egg whites • 2¼ oz/60 g icing sugar

This very light dessert melts in the mouth like ice-cream. The recipe given here is not excessively sweet: the quantity of sugar used can be increased according to taste.

Using the same method, flavoured mousses can be prepared: mousses are always very soft in texture and usually have one dominant flavour, from which they take their name. Some of the varieties of mousse are: melon mousse, orange mousse, strawberry mousse, mandarin mousse, gooseberry mousse, pineapple mousse, lemon mousse, pear mousse, pistachio and strawberry mousse, rice and grape mousse, mousse with liqueur, zabaione mousse, coffee mousse, cinnamon mousse, wine mousse and so on.

1 Line the base and sides of a cake tin with greaseproof paper oiled on both sides.

2 Beat the cream cheese with a wooden spoon until creamy (this is more easily done if the cheese is removed from the refrigerator an hour or two before it is needed).

3 Soften the gelatine in a little hot milk. Pour the rest of the hot milk on to the softened gelatine.

4 Stir into the cream cheese and mix until smooth.

5 Mix in the following ingredients in the order given: the whipped cream, grated lemon rind, lemon juice and liqueur.

6 Whip the egg whites in a separate bowl until firm and add the sugar gradually while still beating.

7 Fold the whipped egg whites carefully into the cream cheese mixture.

8 Pour into the cake tin and chill in the refrigerator for 3-4 hours before unmoulding on to a cold serving dish.

Chocolate mousse

4 egg yolks ● 3½ oz/100 g sugar ● juice of 1 orange ● 3½ oz/100 g cooking chocolate ● knob of butter ● 2 tbsp Marsala or strong coffee ● 1 oz/25 g candied orange peel (see page 187) ● 3 egg whites ● 7 fl oz/200 ml double cream

Chocolate mousse differs from all the other types of mousse in that it does not contain the classic ingredients of a mousse: gelatine or cornflour, or milk. When chocolate is melted and allowed to cool it sets the mousse and no other setting agent is needed.

1 In a pan beat together the egg yolks and the sugar.

2 Place the pan over a low heat, add the orange juice and stir until thickened.

3 Melt the chocolate with the butter and the Marsala or coffee in a bain marie.

4 Stir the chocolate into the egg and orange mixture.

5 Add the candied orange peel.

6 Whisk the egg whites until firm.

7 Fold carefully into the chocolate until the mixture is well blended.

8 Pour into individual dishes or glasses and decorate with a layer of double or whipped cream. Place in the refrigerator until ready to serve.

Cream cheese mousse with bilberries

4 oz/125 g bilberries • 2 tbsp Maraschino • 1 tsp vanilla sugar • ½ tsp salt • 5 oz/150 g cream or curd cheese • 2 tbsp cornflour or potato flour • 2½ oz/70 g icing sugar • 3½ fl oz/100 ml double cream • 3 egg whites

1 Soak the bilberries in a cup with the liqueur and vanilla sugar.

2 Add the salt to the cheese and stir.

3 Add the cornflour and mix well.

4 Stir in the icing sugar, sprinkling it in gradually through a sieve.

5 Whip the cream until stiff.

6 Whip the egg whites until stiff.

7 Fold the egg whites carefully into the whipped cream.

8 Fold this mixture into the cream cheese.

9 Pour the mousse into individual dishes.

10 Place in the refrigerator until needed and decorate each portion with a spoonful of bilberries just before serving.

Vanilla soufflé

14 fl oz/400 ml milk • 3½ oz/100 g sugar • ½ tsp vanilla essence • 1¼ oz/35 g flour • ½ tsp salt • 1 oz/25 g butter • 5 egg yolks • 5 egg whites • butter to grease and sugar to dust dish

Soufflé is a French word which has become an international culinary term; not only the name but the recipe, or recipes, are typical of French cookery. The words itself means 'puffed up'; soufflés are frequently savoury as well as sweet. This is the basic recipe for sweet soufflés which can be varied by adding chocolate, coffee, vanilla, orange liqueur; fruits such as orange, lemon, apricot, strawberries, black cherries, raspberries, peaches, plums, bananas, and so on. When fruit is added it is puréed first.

1 Boil the milk (reserving about 4 fl oz/125 ml) with the sugar and vanilla essence. Leave to stand for 15 minutes.

2 Stir the remaining milk into the flour and salt, then stir this mixture into the flavoured milk.

3 Return to the heat and bring to the boil. Add the butter and allow to cool completely.

4 Beat the egg yolks into the mixture, one by one. Whisk the egg whites and fold in carefully.

5 Pour into a buttered sugared soufflé dish. Alternatively, pour into small individual moulds.

6 Cook in a preheated oven at 325°F/170°C/mark 3. Allow 30-35 minutes for a large soufflé, or 15 minutes for small ones.

Vanilla ice-cream
Coffee ice-cream

For the vanilla ice-cream: 7 fl oz/200 ml milk • 5 fl oz/150 ml double cream • few drops vanilla essence • 3 egg yolks • 2 oz/50 g icing sugar
For the coffee ice-cream: the same ingredients as above (including the vanilla) plus 1 tbsp instant coffee

1 For the vanilla ice-cream boil the milk; for the coffee ice-cream boil the milk and coffee. All the other stages are the same for both ice-creams.

2 Remove from the heat, let cool slightly, add the cream and vanilla essence and allow to cool for at least 15 minutes.

3 In a separate bowl beat together the egg yolks and sugar until pale and creamy.

4 Combine the egg yolks and sugar with the mixture from step 2, stirring constantly.

5 Place the mixture over a very low heat. (If the mixture boils the eggs will curdle and make the mixture unusable.) Stir constantly until thick.

6 Remove from the heat, transfer to a clean bowl and stir until cool.

7 Pour the mixture into an ice-cream mould or shallow dish and keep in the freezer.

Mint sorbet
Orange sorbet

For the mint sorbet: 3½ oz/100 g sugar ● 3½ fl oz/100 ml water ●
3 tbsp lemon juice ● 3 tbsp mint syrup or strong infusion of fresh
mint leaves ● 2 egg whites
For the orange sorbet: 3½ oz/100 g sugar ● ½ pt/300 ml orange
juice ● 2 tbsp kirsch or Maraschino ● 2 egg whites

1 For the mint sorbet (steps 1-6): dissolve the sugar in the water over a low heat. Stir until boiling point is reached then remove from the heat.

2 Add the lemon juice and the mint syrup and stir.

3 Whisk the egg whites until stiff and fold into the mixture.

4 Place in a shallow container and freeze for 2 hours.

5 Remove and stir vigorously at intervals to avoid large crystals from forming as the sorbet freezes.

6 Replace in the freezer to harden and leave until ready to serve.

7 For the orange sorbet: dissolve the sugar in the orange juice over a low heat, stirring until thick. Remove from the heat and add the liqueur. Whisk the egg whites and fold in carefully. Place in a container in the freezer for 2 hours. Remove at intervals and beat until smooth. Replace in the freezer until ready to serve.

Lemon sorbet

3¾ oz/110 g sugar ● 6 fl oz/175 ml water ● 1 tsp arrowroot ●
juice of 4 lemons ● 2 egg whites

The word *sorbet* comes from the Turkish *serbet*, which is derived from the Arab word *sarbat* meaning 'iced drink'. In Turkish the word *serbet* is applied to a great range of iced drinks with a fruit juice or syrup base. These drinks are sometimes thickened (with egg white, for instance) and then frozen in the freezer or refrigerator.

According to taste, a sorbet can be accompanied by a sweet or dry liqueur, or by champagne.

1 Dissolve the sugar in the water over a low heat stirring constantly until syrupy. Remove from the heat.

2 Add the arrowroot and lemon juice and stir well.

3 Whisk the egg whites until stiff and fold carefully into the mixture.

4 Place in a container in the freezer and leave to harden for 2 hours.

5 Stir vigorously at intervals while the mixture is freezing to prevent large crystals from forming.

6 Return to the freezer until set and leave until ready to serve.

Dessert cup

1 part red wine • 1 part sparkling white wine
To decorate: slices of apple

No desserts book is complete without at least one fruit cup. This one is simple yet unusual and brings to mind other world-famous drinks. Everyone is familiar with *sangria* from Spain, Irish coffee, Mexico's *tequila caliente* (with tequila, lemon juice, soda, grenadine and cassis); Russian *kwass* (prepared from dark bread fermented with water, sugar, yeast, raisins, and lemon juice, and filtered before being drunk); the different varieties of Brazilian *batida*; the *Cuba libre* (rum, lemon juice and Coca-Cola). Two curious anecdotes: the Prussian *pillkaller* is a grain spirit which is drunk over a slice of liver sausage spread with mustard. This is kept in the mouth while the spirit is drunk and is then eaten. An Indian 17th-century legend links the English word *punch* with the Indian word *panj*, meaning five. Punch traditionally contained five ingredients. Indian tea punch does in fact contain five ingredients: tea, red wine, rum, orange juice and sugar.

Basic recipes, useful hints and cooking terms

Almond paste

1 lb/500 g almonds • 1 lb/500 g caster sugar • 2 oz/50 g liquid glucose or 3½ oz/100 g honey

Soak the almonds in boiling water for a few minutes until their skins loosen and can be peeled off easily.

Peel and place in a warm oven to dry and toast; toast only until very lightly coloured. (If they are toasted too much they develop a burnt flavour and are no longer suitable for almond paste.) Grind in a blender to obtain a fine flour.

Dissolve the sugar and glucose or honey in a pan and boil until the hard ball stage is reached. See *Sugar syrups*.

Mix together the sugar syrup, which could still be hot, and the ground almonds on a marble slab or in a mortar to form a coarse paste. Continue to work until the paste is cool enough to be handled, then knead as if kneading bread dough, dusting with icing sugar instead of flour. The paste can be made thinner by rolling it through the rollers of a pasta-making machine.

Store in a cool place (not in the refrigerator) in a glass jar; to prevent it from drying out add a little coconut butter.

If you want to use the almond paste at once it must be left to stand for at least 2 hours. In this case the addition of coconut butter is not necessary.

Almond paste is often coloured with natural colourings, and flavoured with liqueurs and essences such as vanilla essence.

Bain marie

See *Cooking in a bain marie*.

Biscuits

The word biscuit (from the French *biscuit* meaning 'twice cooked') originally referred to bread which was cooked twice: first the loaf was baked, then it was sliced and baked again to get rid of all moisture so that it could be kept for longer. The resulting biscuits were used as a substitute for bread. Nowadays, the word biscuit is used to describe shortbread, cookies, crackers and so on.

Commercial biscuits, which are sold in vast quantities today, are usually sweet and are made with water, flour, butter, sugar, eggs and natural flavourings. Biscuits are quite easy to make: the ingredients must, however, be weighed carefully. Other points to remember are that the biscuits should be cut to the same size, to ensure even cooking. Baking trays with very low edges must be used (high sides prevent the biscuits from browning evenly). The biscuits should be baked in the centre of the oven if only one baking tray is being used; if two trays are being baked at the same time plenty of space should be allowed between them. Among the different types of biscuits are:

Slices: the dough is baked in one piece and cut into slices or squares when cooked.

Drops: made with dough which is too soft to be rolled with a rolling pin. The dough is spooned on to the baking tray or piped through a piping bag with a plain nozzle.

Shapes: the biscuits are cut out with a fancy cutter or shaped by hand.

Piped biscuits: the dough is piped through a confectioner's syringe or piping bag, according to the shape required.

Refrigerator biscuits: the dough for these biscuits is usually rolled into a cylinder and kept for several days in the refrigerator or freezer: when quite firm it is sliced off or shaped into thin biscuits and baked.

Flat biscuits: these are rolled out as a sheet of dough and cut with fancy cutters into thin biscuits.

Fancy biscuits: these may be decorated with chocolate or glacé icing, walnuts, almonds, candied fruit, jam, vanilla sugar, granulated sugar or icing sugar.

Iced biscuits: these are iced all over with chocolate, glacé or other icing.

Filled biscuits: these biscuits, either sweet or savoury, are sandwiched together with cream cheese, jam, vanilla or flavoured creams, fruit paste (made from figs, raisins, fresh fruit); the tops may be decorated with chopped nuts, desiccated coconut, and so on.

Biscuits keep best in an airtight tin lined with greaseproof paper, or in the freezer wrapped in foil. (Never put dry and soft biscuits together in the same tin: the moisture from the soft biscuits will soften the crisp biscuits.)

Brioche dough

½ oz/15 g fresh yeast • 2 fl oz/60 ml orange flower water or milk • 10½ oz/300 g flour • 7 oz/200 g butter • 1¼ oz/35 g sugar • 1 tsp salt • 3 eggs

Moisten the yeast with the orange flower water and add one-sixth of the flour. Leave in a warm place until doubled in volume.

Cream the butter. Mix together the remaining flour, the sugar and the salt, add the eggs and mix to a dough. Incorporate the yeast and finally the butter. Cover the bowl and leave the dough to rise for about 10 hours, until doubled in volume. Brush the brioche moulds with oil and fill half full with the dough. Make a hole in the centre with your finger and place a small ball of dough over each hole. Brush the brioches with beaten egg. Bake in a preheated oven at 450°F/230°C/mark 8 for 10-20 minutes until golden brown. Remove from the oven and turn out immediately to cool.

Buttercream

7 oz/200 g butter • 7 oz/200 g sugar • 4 egg yolks • 2 egg whites (optional)

Cream the butter and sugar together until smooth and light. Add the egg yolks one by one, stirring continuously. Whisk the egg whites separately and fold gently into the mixture. This is the basic recipe for buttercream. Other buttercreams contain additional ingredients for example vanilla buttercream (add vanilla essence); liqueur buttercream (add 1-2 tbsp rum or other liqueur); hazelnut buttercream (the nuts are toasted and finely ground before being added); pistachio buttercream; almond buttercream; lemon buttercream (add 1 tbsp lemon juice); chocolate buttercream (add 3 oz/80 g melted chocolate); coffee buttercream (add 2-3 tbsp strong black coffee; see also page 19, steps 5 and 6); Torinese buttercream (with ground pralined almonds and melted chocolate); pistachio and Grand Marnier buttercream.

Candied fruit

Wash and peel the fruit. Simmer the fruit, citrus peel or chestnuts in water until tender. (Citrus peel requires at least 2 hours' cooking.)

1 *Pestle and mortar* for crushing toasted nuts, either roughly or into a fine flour. Electric grinders have more or less replaced the pestle and mortar in the modern kitchen. The pestle is also useful for reducing cooked foods to a pulp.

2 *Cake tin* for all kinds of cakes; available in many sizes.

3 *Small saucepan* with rounded sides and a thick copper base, useful for preparing creams and for melting sugar, chocolate, and so on.

4 *Dariole mould* for individual cream caramels and rum babas.

5 *Rectangular fluted mould* for ice-creams and iced desserts. The shape makes the cutting of even slices very simple.

6 *Brushes* of various sizes for brushing cakes or pastry with egg or melted butter before baking.

7 *Balloon whisk* for hand beating and for whisking egg whites, whipping cream, and so on.

8 *Spring-release cake tin* for delicate cakes which are difficult to turn out without breaking.

9 *Metal scoops* for serving portions of ice-cream, or for removing the flesh from melons and water melons for fruit salads.

10 *Flan tin* with fluted edges and decorated base, for tarts and pies.

11 *Metal tubes* for fashioning tubes of pastry.

12 *Large metal tubes* for moulding and cooking tubes of dough and pastry.

13 *Pastry wheel* for cutting out biscuits and decorations and for dividing up sheets of pastry.

14 *Piping bag and nozzles* for decorating. The bag is filled with cream and used for decorating cakes and sweetmeats. It can also be filled with biscuit dough, or meringue, or with icing or caramel for decorating desserts. A wide variety of nozzles give different decorative effects.

15 *Heat-resistant ramekins* (these are sometimes made of glass) for soufflés, mousses, miniature charlottes, iced desserts, and so on.

16 *Pastry cutters* in various shapes and sizes, for biscuits and decorations.

Prepare a sugar syrup and bring to the boil. Place the fruit in the syrup and bring to the boil again. Remove from the heat and leave for at least 24 hours.

Repeat this operation, adding another 2 oz/50 g sugar to the syrup and allowing the fruit to stand for at least 24 hours. Repeat the operation for a third time, with a final 2 oz/50 g sugar. Leave the fruit in the syrup for 24 hours. Drain the fruit and dry it on a wire rack.

Caramelized fruit

3½ oz/100 g liquid glucose to every 1 lb/500 g fruit of your choice

Fresh and dried fruit can be caramelized by dipping them in sugar syrup at the caramel stage, allowing the caramel to harden, and then dipping the fruit in the caramel again.

Candied fruit and citrus peel can also be caramelized (see page 88). Candied or dried fruit (dates in particular) can be sandwiched with a filling such as almond paste before being caramelized. See *Almond paste* and see also page 84.

Chantilly cream

½ pint/300 ml double cream ● 1 oz/25 g icing sugar

Whip the cream until it forms peaks. Fold in the sugar carefully.

Chantilly cream is also often called 'sweetened whipped cream'.

In spite of extensive research no one has conclusively established why Chantilly cream is so named. Chantilly is a town in northern France famous for lace and pottery, and the invention of sweetened whipped cream is often attributed to the chef Vatel who worked for many years in the Château de Chantilly; some maintain that it was invented by the Sicilian pastry-cook Procopio dei Coltelli; both lived in the 17th century.

One story maintains, however, that the name

Chantilly was first used in Rome when troops from Chantilly were occupying the town; they allegedly introduced the cream.

Chestnuts

Cooking chestnuts: Prick each chestnut with the point of a knife. Heat them over a flame in a chestnut pan with holes in it until their shells and skins come off easily. Boil them in salted milk (1 tsp salt to each pint/600 ml of milk) or water. Add more milk if necessary while the chestnuts are cooking. The chestnuts should be cooked when the milk has been almost completely absorbed — at least 45 minutes. Drain the chestnuts and allow them to cool completely.

Chocolate-covered chestnuts: Dip cooked, cooled chestnuts in melted chocolate to which sugar has been added (see *Chocolate*) and allow the chocolate to harden. Chocolate chestnuts are usually used for decoration or as a filling.

Chocolate chestnut truffles: A variation on the chocolate chestnuts described above, these are simple to make and are usually used for decoration, or for eating as sweets. Heat 1 lb/500 g chestnuts over a flame in a chestnut pan with holes in it until they can be shelled and peeled with ease. Boil then in salted water until tender, drain them and press them through a food mill. Mix with 3½ oz/100 g finely grated chocolate, 2-3 tbsp whipped cream, 3-6 tbsp sugar (according to sweetness desired) and a few drops of vanilla essence. Form into balls the size of walnuts, roll in cocoa powder mixed with sugar and allow to harden in the refrigerator. Serve in pleated paper cups.

Caramelized chestnuts: (See *Caramelized fruit*).

Chocolate

Melting chocolate: Grate or break the chocolate into small pieces. Place in a

heat-resistant bowl or pan over another pan of simmering water over a low heat. If the chocolate remains very thick or lumpy, add a little margarine or butter and lower the heat. If you have no chocolate, but only cocoa powder, proceed in the same way with the following quantities and ingredients: 3 parts cocoa to 1 part margarine.

To make decorations out of chocolate, pour the melted chocolate on to a clean marble slab and work with a spatula until cold and firm. Cut into squares or shapes. See also *Cocoa*.

Chocolate cream

3 egg whites ● 3½ oz/100 g sugar syrup ● 7 oz/200 g chocolate buttercream

Whisk the egg whites until very stiff. Fold in the freshly prepared sugar syrup (see *Sugar syrups*).

Finally mix with the chocolate buttercream (see *Buttercream*). This cream is often used as a filling for chocolate cakes. See also page 21, steps 6 and 7.

Cocoa

Cocoa powder is extracted from the seeds of the fruit of the cocoa plant, originally found in tropical America but now grown in tropical regions all over the world. The fruit or pod of the cocoa plant can be as long as 8-10 in/20-25 cm and can contain as many as 50 seeds.

The process of extracting the cocoa is very complicated: the seeds are left to ferment in the open air or underground, then they are washed, dried, roasted, fermented a second time and ground. At this stage a large proportion of the cocoa butter is separated from the seeds (the seeds contain a large quantity of oils and fats which are used for cosmetics and medicines, as well as for making chocolate).

Cocoa is very widely used in pâtisserie and confectionery. Dissolved with sugar and milk it makes a hot chocolate drink, which

can be served with whipped cream; it is also used to make chocolate which is produced by heating together cocoa powder with cocoa butter and by adding different proportions of sugar and milk. The mixture is allowed to set in various shapes and thickness.

The main use of cocoa is in the manufacture of chocolate. Solid chocolate must always be melted before it can be used to cover or ice items of pâtisserie or confectionery.

Confectioner's custard

9 fl oz/250 ml milk ● 9 fl oz/250 ml single cream ● 1 tsp grated lemon or orange rind, or 1 tsp vanilla essence ● 6 oz/175 g sugar ● 1 tsp cornflour or potato flour ● 10 egg yolks

Place the milk (reserving one glassful) and cream in a pan over a low heat. Flavour with the orange or lemon rind, or the vanilla essence. Add the sugar gradually, stirring constantly.

Mix the flour with half the egg yolks then stir in the reserved cold milk.

When the flavoured milk is about to boil add the flour and egg yolk mixture; stir constantly and remove from heat before boiling point is reached.

Pour the mixture through a sieve into a clean bowl. Continue to stir, add the remaining egg yolks and allow to cool. The custard may be flavoured by adding 3½ oz/100 g melted chocolate or cocoa powder.

See also page 15, steps 1-4.

Cooking in a bain marie

The cooking of liquids or solids in a receptacle partially immersed in simmering water; the temperature of the food being cooked never reaches boiling point. This method is generally used for cooking sauces or keeping them hot, for custards and egg dishes and in all cases where it is important to prevent overheating or curdling. The receptacle containing the food to be cooked must be smaller than the pan containing the water. The latter should be no more than half full so that there is no risk of water splashing into the smaller pan.

The term 'bain marie' comes from the name of its supposed inventor, Mary the Alchemist, sister of Moses and Aaron.

Cooking in the oven

When a 'cool oven' is indicated, this means a temperature between 250° - 300°F/130° - 150°C/ mark ½-2. A 'warm to moderate oven' means from 350°-400°F/180°-200°C/mark 4-6. A 'very hot oven' means from 400° - 475°F/200° - 240°C/ mark 6-9.

The oven must always be preheated before the cake or dessert is put in to cook. Never put things into a cold oven unless instructed to do so, and never leave the cake or dessert waiting (particularly with yeast dough) while the oven warms up. The timing of the preparation and the preheating of the oven must be carefully planned.

Before being placed in the oven baking trays and tins are usually buttered and dusted with flour, or with fine breadcrumbs; alternatively they may be brushed with oil or lined with baking parchment.

During cooking the oven should not be opened as the temperature will drop and cakes and soufflés in particular might be ruined. If it is absolutely unavoidable (or if the recipe instructs you to do so) open the door carefully, avoiding sudden draughts of air, and close it as quickly as possible.

Cream cheese filling

3½ oz/100 g icing sugar • 1 egg yolk • 3½ oz/100 g cream cheese or curd cheese • 1 tbsp liqueur of your choice • 1 egg white

Beat the sugar and the egg yolk until pale. Add the cheese and liqueur. Whisk the egg white until stiff and fold carefully into the cream, stirring from bottom to top.

Chocolate or coffee can be added to this cream. By increasing the number of egg yolks or the quantity of liqueur, or by adding more egg whites you can achieve an extremely light cream, which can often be used instead of confectioner's custard or buttercream.

Croissant dough

½ oz/15 g fresh yeast • 2 fl oz/60 ml milk or orange flower water • 10½ oz/ 300 g flour • 1 oz/25 g sugar • 1 tsp salt • 1 whole egg • 1 egg yolk • 3½ fl oz/100 ml milk • 6 oz/175 g softened butter • 1 egg beaten with 1 tsp icing sugar to glaze • butter to grease and flour to dust baking tray

Mix the yeast with the milk and a few tbsp flour. Leave to rise until doubled in volume. Make a dough with the remaining flour, the sugar, salt, whole egg and egg yolk, the milk and 2 oz/50 g butter. Work in the yeast and leave to rise until the dough has doubled in volume (overnight if possible). Roll out the dough with a rolling pin. Spread the remaining softened butter over two-thirds of the dough with a spatula, fold the dough in three and roll out with the rolling pin. Leave to rest in a cool place for 15 minutes. Fold in three again and flatten again with the rolling pin. Leave to rest for another 15 minutes. Roll out the pastry to ¾ in/2 cm and cut into isosceles triangles. Roll these up, beginning at the base and shape into crescents. Place on a buttered, floured baking tray. Brush with egg and icing sugar beaten together and bake in a preheated oven at 450°F/ 230°C/mark 8 for 20 minutes. Most croissants sold nowadays are made with flaky pastry; those made

according to the recipe given here are brioches shaped into crescents — as were the original French croissants.

Custard

5 fl oz/150 ml milk • 2 oz/50 g icing sugar • 1 tbsp flour • 1 tbsp potato flour or cornflour • 2 egg yolks • ½ oz/15 g butter

Scald the milk. Add the sugar, flour and potato flour and cook gently, stirring, until the mixture thickens. Remove from the heat and add the egg yolks and butter, beating vigorously. Allow to cool. Custard is sometimes flavoured with a few drops of vanilla essence. See also page 48 step 2.

Deep frying

The pan for deep frying should always have high sides so that both the oil and the food being fried fit comfortably inside (the oil must not overflow when it boils).

Fried sweetmeats are usually cooked in lard or oil, the latter being preferred nowadays. Most suitable is seed oil which is light and economical.

When you are deep frying care must be taken with the fat or oil, with what you are frying and how you fry it. It is important therefore to know the different degrees of heat used when frying:

moderate fat: using a low heat, slow but steady; for food which needs to be cooked inside before the outside becomes too crisp or begins to burn.

hot fat: with constant, moderate heat underneath, used for sweetmeats which are already partly cooked, then coated in batter; the aim is to cook the outside until crisp and golden.

very hot fat: using high heat for very small pieces of food which must cook at once, without burning.

A very important point to remember when deep frying is to wait until the oil is hot; if it is not hot enough it soaks into the food and

makes it soggy, preventing a golden and crisp finish.

Frangipane cream

2 egg yolks • 2 oz/50 g sugar • 4 tbsp flour • 4 tbsp ground almonds • 3½ fl oz/100 ml milk • few drops vanilla essence

Beat the egg yolks and sugar until pale and creamy. Add the flour and the ground almonds (see *Ground almonds*). Stir in the milk and vanilla essence. Press through a sieve to remove lumps. Place in a pan over a low heat and stir until very thick and smooth. See also pages 82-3, steps 12-16.

Fruit in syrup

1 lb/500 g fresh fruit • 3½ oz/100 g sugar • 3½ fl oz/100 ml brandy or wine • 3½ fl oz/100 ml water

Cook all the ingredients (the alcohol is optional but if it is omitted double the quantity of water) over a very low heat until the sugar has dissolved and thickened to form a syrup and the fruit is tender.

Fruit jellies

The method by which jelly is made is similar to jam making, but for jelly only the juice of the fruit is used. Where the juice of the fruit is difficult to extract from the fruit use the following method: clean the fruit (cut into pieces if necessary), place in a pan and cover with water. Simmer until soft, then strain through a fine sieve.

Place the juice with an equal weight of sugar in a pan on a low heat. While it is cooking, skim frequently with a slotted spoon (this is important: you will not obtain a clear jelly unless you skim carefully). Setting point is reached when drops of jelly stick to the spoon as it is lifted from the pan.

Fruit juice

The juice of citrus fruits is easy to extract with the

help of the various squeezers on the market which keep the juice separate from the pith and pips. Very soft fruits, such as strawberries and raspberries can be puréed in a blender, or passed through a nylon sieve.

Electric juice extractors are available in the shops for hard fruits (such as pears and apples) where the juice is difficult to extract. Alternatively, cut the fruit into small pieces and cook in a little water with lemon juice, then sieve or purée as for other fruit.

Fruit syrups

To obtain fruit syrup make a light sugar syrup but use fruit instead of water. See *Sugar syrups*.

Glazes

Honey glaze: Melt the honey over a low heat with a few spoonfuls of water.
Honey glaze with liqueur: To the above add a few drops of the liqueur of your choice and stir until well blended and slightly reduced. The spirit most often used is rum (see page 61, step 3): white rum for a pale glaze, dark rum for a dark glaze.
Jam glaze: Melt a few tbsp of jam over a low heat: the jam becomes more liquid and is easier to brush, while still warm, over sponge or other pâtisserie. For a thinner glaze, dilute the jam with a little water. The jams most frequently used in baking are apricot, which gives a golden glaze, and raspberry which gives a reddish glaze, (choose seedless raspberry jam or sieve it to remove seeds). Fruit jelly can be used as a glaze in the same way.
Rum glaze: Melt icing sugar in a pan over low heat. Add a few drops of rum (or other liqueurs) and stir to blend.

Ground almonds

Almonds and hazelnuts, peanuts and walnuts can be ground to a fine meal for use in cakes, puddings and sauces.

Place the almonds in boiling water for 5 minutes, to loosen their skins. Peel them, then place in a preheated oven to toast (they should not be allowed to burn as this makes them bitter and unusable). They can then be ground either coarsely or finely, according to the use for which they are required.
Toasted in the oven whole (or halved), with a little salt, almonds make an excellent accompaniment to aperitifs.

Ice-creams and sorbets

The basic ingredients of ice-cream are sugar, eggs, milk or cream and the flavourings which give the ice-cream its name (vanilla, chocolate, lemon, strawberry, nougat and so on). These ingredients are cooked then set by freezing and so the exact proportion of the ingredients (4 oz/125 g sugar, 4 eggs, 18 fl oz/500 ml milk) is vitally important if the result is to be neither gritty (when too little sugar is used), nor difficult to freeze (if too much sugar is used).
A sorbet is made by freezing a flavouring such as a fruit purée with a sugar syrup and whipped egg whites.

Icing

Icing is used to cover gâteaux and buns (a soft icing is required in this case so that there is sufficient time before it hardens to spread it evenly); it is also used to decorate all kinds of cakes (in this case the icing should be thick so that it does not drip).
Icing can also be called 'glazing', (from the English word 'glass' and the French 'glacé', meaning ice or glass). However, the term glazing also includes glazing with jam or syrup.
Glacé icing: Sieve icing sugar into a bowl (this should always be done before making any type of icing); add hot water gradually, stirring, until you have a thick smooth paste. Use immediately.

Variations to glacé icing can be made by adding different flavourings: cocoa powder, melted chocolate, coffee, a few drops of Grand Marnier (see page 25) or other liqueurs, orange or lemon juice, caramel and so on.
Weeping icing: This is made in the same way as ordinary glacé icing, but with more water so that it is thinner. It is used where a very thin, fluid effect is required.
Royal icing: Use 1 egg white per 5 oz/150 g icing sugar. Sift the sugar gradually into the lightly beaten egg white. Add a few drops of lemon juice to make the icing whiter.
Royal icing will keep in a tightly sealed glass container and when needed it can be softened on the stove, with the addition of a little water if necessary.
Fondant icing: Often simply called 'fondant', this is in many ways the best icing, not least because it will keep almost indefinitely.
Melt sugar with liquid glucose or cream of tartar (1 tsp to every 10½ oz/300 g sugar) in a pan; boil until the soft ball stage is reached (see *Sugar syrups*). Sprinkle cold water on a marble slab or work surface. Pour the syrup on to the slab and work it until it is opaque and stiff. Before using the fondant for icing, reheat it and dilute it with a little water.
Jam: Jam and fruit jelly, though made from the same ingredients (fruit and sugar), are not the same product. Jam is made with pieces of fruit, or whole fruits if they are small enough (cherries for example). Jelly is made purely from the juice of the fruit cooked with sugar. See *Glazes*.

Lemon cream

The base of this recipe is confectioner's custard, using lemon juice instead of the lemon rind or vanilla. It is used as a filling for cakes. See *Confectioner's custard* and also page 44, steps 2-3.

Liqueur-flavoured syrups

¾ pt/450 ml water ● 6 oz/175 g sugar ● 5 fl oz/150 ml rum, kirsch or other liqueur

Boil the sugar and water together until the short thread stage is reached (see *Sugar syrups*). Let the syrup cool a little, then stir in the liqueur. Grand Marnier and Maraschino syrups are made in the same way.

Marzipan

1 lb/500 g caster sugar ● 5 fl oz/150 ml water ● pinch of cream of tartar ● ¾ lb/350 g ground almonds ● 2 egg whites ● 2¾ oz/75 g icing sugar

Marzipan and almond paste are very similar but not identical; they are therefore often confused one with the other (see *Almond Paste*).
Almond paste is used mainly as a filling for cakes and biscuits. Marzipan is used mainly for decoration. Dissolve the caster sugar in a pan with the water, stirring constantly. Add the cream of tartar. Bring to the boil without stirring until the soft ball stage is reached (see *Sugar syrups*). Remove from the heat and stir. Add the ground almonds and beaten egg whites. Stir once, return to the heat for a few minutes and continue to stir. Turn on to a lightly oiled marble (or formica) surface. Add the icing sugar and work the paste with a spatula, bringing the outside edge to the centre. When cool enough to work by hand knead until smooth (add a little more icing sugar if necessary).
This marzipan can be used either in a single sheet to decorate larger cakes or it can be shaped and coloured in a variety of ways with natural or synthetic food colourings. It is often moulded into fruits which are then glazed.

Meringue

2 egg whites • 4 oz/125 g icing sugar

Meringue can be a dessert on its own or it can be used for decorating (by means of a piping bag) or for topping (with a spatula) different cakes and desserts.
Whisk the egg whites until they form peaks. Add the icing sugar gradually, letting it fall through a sieve to eliminate lumps. Fold the sugar in carefully, stirring from bottom to top to prevent the egg whites collapsing.
It is useful to remember that meringue browns in less than 10 minutes in an oven set at 400°F/200°C/mark 6, so if it is being used as a decoration or topping on a cake or flan the meringue should be added only for the final 10 minutes.
If the meringue is used as a filling the above advice does not apply.
A meringue mixture can be enriched with other ingredients such as ground almonds or ground hazelnuts. See also page 173, page 44 and page 167.

Nozzles

For decorating cakes and desserts with whipped cream, icing or buttercream you need a confectioner's syringe or piping bag and a set of nozzles; each nozzle will produce a different patterned effect.
The different nozzles include:

Plain nozzle: for making drops, blobs, dots and for writing and drawing.

Star or pointed nozzle: for making stars, rosettes and shells.

Petal nozzle: for decorative scrolls and ribbons and delicate flower designs.

Flower nozzle: for making small flowers.

Leaf nozzle: for making delicate leaf and flower designs.

Orange cream

3½ oz/100 g sugar • 3½ fl oz/100 ml orange juice • 2 egg yolks • 7 fl oz/200 ml whipped cream

Dissolve the sugar in the orange juice in a bain marie. Add the yolks and stir until the mixture thickens. Do not overheat. Remove from the heat and fold in the cream, stirring carefully from bottom to top so that the whipped cream does not collapse. See also page 91, step 8.

Pastry cream

6 egg yolks • 5 oz/150 g icing sugar • 2 oz/50 g flour • 18 fl oz/500 ml milk • few drops vanilla essence or piece of lemon peel

Beat the egg yolks and sugar in a bowl until pale. Continuing to beat, add the flour through a sieve, then the milk. Place over a low heat, add the lemon peel or vanilla essence and stir until the mixture has thickened to the required custard consistency. Remove from the heat and discard the lemon peel if used; melt a knob of butter on the surface of the pastry cream to prevent a skin from forming while it cools. For a zabaione-flavoured cream a small glass of dry Marsala can be added. Alternatively add 2 oz/50 g grated chocolate or cocoa powder for chocolate pastry cream.

Pralined nuts

7 oz/200 g nuts (almonds, walnuts, hazelnuts or peanuts) • 7 oz/200 g caster sugar

Using a clean cloth wipe any loose dust from the nuts. Place the sugar and a few tbsp water in a pan over a low heat; when the sugar has begun to caramelize (see *Sugar syrups*) add the nuts; mix with a wooden spoon until the nuts are covered in white granules.
Tip the nuts on to a marble surface to cool. If small pieces of praline are required, crush with a rolling pin.

Preserves

This general term is used to describe several different kinds of preserve:
jellies: fruit juice reduced with sugar to a jelly; occasionally set with a minimal amount of gelatine or pectin.
jams: whole or chopped fruit or peel cooked with sugar.
conserves and pickles: vegetables in tins or jars (preserved in brine, oil or vinegar) and spicy chutneys made from fruit and vegetables with added garlic, onions, pepper, mustard, vinegar, and so on.
Tinned or bottled fruit in syrup (used in some of the recipes in this book) can also be considered preserves.

Puff and flaky pastry

1 lb/500 g butter • 1 lb/500 g flour • 1 tsp salt • 2½ fl oz/75 ml cold water or dry white wine • 1 beaten egg to glaze • butter to grease and sugar to dust baking tray

Take the butter out of the refrigerator 2 hours before it is needed. Pour the flour into a bowl and add the salt. Work a quarter of the butter into the flour. Add the water or wine and make a dough.
Roll out the dough with a rolling pin into a rectangle three times as long as it is wide. Spread the butter across two-thirds of the surface of the dough.
Fold the dough into three, making sure that the unbuttered third is in the middle (i.e. between the two buttered thirds).
Press the edges together with the rolling pin or by hand to prevent the butter squeezing out.
Roll the pastry out into a rectangle as before: fold in three again, wrap in cling film and chill in the refrigerator for 30 minutes. Repeat this operation twice for quick flaky pastry or five times for genuine puff pastry (which is better).
Butter a rectangular baking tray and dust with sugar (or use a round tray for cakes with layers of flaky pastry). Place the pastry on the baking tray, brush with beaten egg and dust with sugar. Bake in a preheated oven at 425°F/220°C/mark 7 for about 15 minutes or until lightly browned.

Raising agents

Yeast: Yeast are microorganisms. The yeasts most generally used in baking are manufactured by allowing dough or molasses to ferment (thus providing the environment for yeast to develop) or as a by-product of brewing beer. Yeast for baking is available either fresh or as dried granules. Yeast is fresh when it is smooth, has a pale colour and acid smell; it can be kept in a cool place wrapped in foil for up to a month or frozen. Use about 1 tbsp yeast for every 1½ lb/700 g flour. If using dried yeast, follow the instructions on the packet.
Baking powder: This is sold ready mixed and is a combination of bicarbonate of soda and cream of tartar. To ensure even distribution of the baking powder, and an evenly risen dough, it is advisable to mix the powder with the flour before adding the liquid.
Dough mixed with a raising agent is left to rest in the refrigerator or in a cool place for several hours; it should then be allowed to return to room temperature before it is used.

Redcurrant and vanilla cream

½ pt/300 ml milk • 2 tbsp sugar • few drops vanilla essence • 1 tsp potato flour or cornflour • 2 tbsp redcurrants (or 1 tbsp redcurrant jelly)

Mix all the ingredients together in a pan and place over a low heat. Bring to the boil and boil gently for a few minutes, stirring constantly. Turn into a large mould or into several small moulds. Allow to cool, then place in the refrigerator.

Royal Paste

9 oz/250 g sugar • 9 oz/250 g ground almonds • pinch of cinnamon • 2 fl oz/60 ml sweet liqueur

Mix together the sugar, ground almonds and cinnamon: add the liqueur and work to a paste. To make the paste smooth stir over a low heat for a few minutes.
This paste can be modelled into different shapes and can be coloured: it should be baked in a moderate oven. Royal paste is often shaped into different fruits. The recipe comes from Sicily where royal paste fruit is called Martorana fruit; the Martorana convent, where the nuns invented this kind of fruit, is in Palermo.
Royal paste is similar to marzipan, but not identical.

Sponge

6 egg yolks • 6 oz/175 g caster sugar • 6 egg whites • 5½ oz/160 g flour • few drops vanilla essence • butter to grease and flour to dust cake tin

Butter a 10-in/25-cm cake tin and dust with flour, turning it upside-down to get rid of excess. Preheat the oven to 325°F/170°C/mark 3.
Beat the egg yolks and sugar in a bowl until light and pale. Whisk the egg whites stiffly using a balloon whisk, and fold into the egg mixture carefully, stirring from bottom to top; sift the flour and add with the vanilla essence to the mixture. Pour into the cake tin and bake for about 40 minutes. See also page 19, steps 1-4.

St-Honoré cream

8 egg yolks • 7 oz/200 g icing sugar • 5 oz/150 g caster sugar • 8 egg whites • 9 fl oz/250 ml milk • 9 fl oz/250 ml

cream • few drops vanilla essence

This cream is generally used only in Gâteau St-Honoré and is a kind of enriched confectioner's custard.
Beat the egg yolks and icing sugar together in a bowl until pale. Place the caster sugar in a pan over a low heat and cook it to the soft ball stage (see Sugar syrups). Whisk the egg whites until stiff.
Place the milk (reserving 1-2 glasses) in a pan with the cream and vanilla essence. Mix the reserved cold milk with the egg yolk and sugar mixture. Add the hot milk gradually, stirring constantly. Return to the heat and stir until almost boiling. Stir in the sugar syrup and carefully fold in the egg whites. Allow to cool, stirring from time to time until cold.
Chocolate St-Honoré cream: Gâteau St-Honoré is often filled and decorated with two different-coloured creams. They are prepared in the same way; the darker one is made by adding melted chocolate or cocoa powder 2-4 oz/50-125 g according to taste.

Sugar syrups

To cook sugar and to make any kind of custard it is best to use a pan with rounded sides (no angles where the sides meet the base).
To prepare a sugar syrup, place the sugar with one-third of its weight in water over a low heat. Stir to dissolve the sugar and bring to the boil.
As a syrup cooks it becomes progressively more concentrated so that first a light syrup is formed, then a heavier one. These syrups are useful for moistening sponge cake and glazing. If the syrup continues to cook and its temperature increases it will go through the changes below. Each stage has particular uses in the making of desserts and sweets.
short thread 223°-236°F/105°-113°C: when a small amount of syrup dropped

from a spoon forms a fine thread as it falls.
soft ball 236°-244°F/113°-118°C: when you roll a piece of syrup, first dipped in cold water, it forms an elastic ball.
hard ball 244°-266°F/118°-130°C: when you repeat the above operation and obtain a harder ball that holds its shape when pressed.
crack 226°-320°F/130°-160°C: when the syrup begins to turn slightly yellow; if you dip a piece into cold water it splutters. It snaps between the fingers rather than bending.
caramel 320°-250°F/160°-177°C: when the syrup turns first a light and then a darker caramel colour. This stage is used for cream caramel and for colouring creams and icing (only a few drops are needed).
To prevent caramel from hardening and to keep it liquid pour some cold water on to it as soon as it has been removed from the heat; then melt it again over a low heat for a few minutes. Do not allow the sugar syrup to cook beyond the caramel stage or it will burn and turn black; it is practically unusable at this stage except for making special kinds of toffees.

Sweet shortcrust pastry

7 oz/200 g flour • 3½ oz/100 g butter • 3½ oz/100 g sugar • 2 eggs • 1 tsp grated lemon rind or few drops vanilla essence • ½ tsp salt

This sweet shortcrust pastry is the basic recipe on which there are several variations: cocoa, ground almonds or hazelnuts can be added.
Shortcrust pastry should be prepared as quickly as possible, otherwise it crumbles when rolled out.
Place the flour, sugar and salt in a heap on the work surface. Make a well in the centre and work in the butter. Add the eggs and flavouring. Work all the ingredients together until a smooth ball of pastry is

obtained. Wrap the pastry in a cloth and leave in a cool place for at least 1 hour. Roll out and bake at 400°F/200°C/mark 6 for about 30 minutes. The quantities given here are sufficient for a 9-in/23-cm flan base, or a 7-in/18-cm pie, 12 small pies or 24 tartlets.
See also pages 39-40, steps 1-7.

Vanilla

When vanilla is listed in a recipe this generally means vanilla essence which is obtained from the vanilla plant, a member of the orchid family. Synthetic vanilla, which is produced chemically, can have a slightly bitter taste. *Vanilla sugar*: To flavour caster or icing sugar with vanilla, keep a vanilla pod in a tightly sealed jar with the sugar.

Walnut cream

4 oz/125 g butter • 4 oz/125 g icing sugar • 3½ oz/100 g ground walnuts • 1 egg yolk • 1 egg white

Take the butter out of the refrigerator 2 hours before it is required so that it is fairly soft.
Using a wooden spoon, cream the butter. Gradually add the sugar and beat until very pale. Stir in the walnuts (see *Ground almonds*) and then the egg yolk.
Whisk the egg white until very stiff and fold into the mixture carefully, stirring from bottom to top so that the egg white does not collapse.
This cream can be used to fill or cover different types of cake. It is occasionally used as the main ingredients of a recipe. See also page 32.

Yeast doughs

Many doughs are prepared with yeast, from brioche dough to pizza bases to cakes.
The most difficult stages with yeast are the kneading

and first rising. If this stage is unsuccessful the results can be disappointing. The recommended flour to use for desserts is best-quality superfine flour with the minimum amount of bran. Even when making dough for sweet buns or breads salt should be added to improve the flavour. If salt is not added, or less than the recommended amount is used, the dough may rise too quickly. Too much salt on the other hand will hinder the rising of the dough and may spoil the texture of the final result. Liquid, usually water or milk, proportionate to the quantity of flour is then added; this should be tepid but the temperature should not exceed 100°F/40°C. If the recipe includes butter or eggs, or both, the amount of liquid required is less; sometimes no additional liquid is needed.

After kneading, the best way of making the dough rise is to place it, covered, in the refrigerator for 12-24 hours. Take the dough out of the refrigerator and allow to rise for a further 2 hours at room temperature. Knead the dough after this first rising, then leave to rise again until doubled in volume in the tin in which it will be cooked. See also *Raising agents*.

Yogurt cream

3 parts confectioner's custard ● 1 part yogurt

Mix the ingredients together. This cream is often used in the Balkans for bavarois and moulds. See *Confectioner's custard*.

Zabaione

For each serving:
1 egg yolk ● 1 tbsp caster sugar ● 2 tbsp dry Marsala

Beat the egg yolk and sugar until pale and fluffy. Add the Marsala gradually, continuing to beat. Prepared in this way zabaione is a dessert in its own right and is often taken as a fortifying pick-me-up. Zabaione can also be made over a low heat, preferably in a bain marie, so that it rises as much as possible. It is then allowed to cool and is served with dessert biscuits or wafers. Zabaione should not be confused with Zabaione cream which is used as a filling for cakes.

Zabaione cream

3 egg yolks ● 3½ oz/100 g icing sugar ● 2 fl oz/60 ml dry Marsala ● ½ pint/300 ml double cream ●

Beat together the egg yolks and sugar. Add the Marsala a spoonful at a time.
Place in a bain marie over low heat and continue beating until light and fluffy. Allow to cool, stirring occasionally.
Whip the cream until very stiff and fold in carefully.

LIST OF RECIPES

PICTURE SOURCES

Maki Irie	13, 28, 180
Ai Kidosaki	14, 26, 37, 42, 43, 60, 63, 64, 66, 79
	84, 85, 92, 122, 133, 169
Katsumi Sakaguchi	16, 17, 18, 24, 34, 36, 38, 45, 46, 72,
	80, 120, 158
Masako Hamano	20
Fusako Holthaus	87, 88, 178, 184
Aiko Ochiai	90, 118, 172, 185
Nobuko Shimizu	168
Reiko Kasai	48, 117, 124, 126
Minako Imada	65, 69, 115
Hisashi Kudo	52, 86, 163, 165, 170, 175, 176, 182, 183
Merry Minami	131, 135, 136, 140, 141, 142, 144, 146, 148
	149, 150, 155, 156, 160
Tokiko Suzuki	95, 97, 98, 100, 102, 103, 104
Eisei Shin	105, 106, 109, 110

Mario Rossi, Milan: pages 22, 23, 27, 30, 31, 32, 33, 49, 50, 51, 57, 58, 61, 68, 70, 76, 89, 113, 128, 134, 166, 167, 173, 181.

Roberto Circià and Giorgio Perego, Vimodrone (Milan): pages 188-189.

The publishers would like to thank Eugenio Medagliani for the loan of equipment for the photograph on pages 188-189.